General Education & Liberal Learning
Principles of Effective Practice

By Paul L. Gaston

*with J. Elizabeth Clark, Ann S. Ferren,
Peggy Maki, Terrel L. Rhodes,
Karen Maitland Schilling, and Dwight Smith*

Association of American Colleges and Universities

Association
of American
Colleges and
Universities

1818 R Street, NW
Washington, DC 20009

Copyright 2010 by the Assocation of American Colleges and Universities.
All rights reserved.

ISBN 978-0-911696-22-6

Table of Contents

Preface v
Acknowledgments vii

Part One: General Education, Liberal Education
Introduction 1
    Terrel L. Rhodes
1. Imperatives for and Drivers of Change 7
    Paul L. Gaston

Part Two: General Education as Curricular Cornerstone
2. Principles of Strong General Education Programs 17
    Paul L. Gaston

Part Three: Effective Practices in General Education
3. Intentionality 25
    Ann S. Ferren
4. Alignment with the Majors 33
    Karen Maitland Schilling and Dwight Smith
5. Effective Pedagogy 39
    J. Elizabeth Clark
6. Assessment 45
    Peggy Maki

Part Four: Sustaining General Education Programs
7. Institutional Commitment 51
    Paul L. Gaston
References 59
About the Author 63

Preface

One of the familiar "Arkansas Traveler" episodes describes a tourist asking a farmer across the fence whether he has lived on the farm all his life. The farmer responds, "not yet." That homely but wise rejoinder may point to the recovery in our time of a view of education first articulated by Socrates, that effective teaching intends not the "filling of a vessel" but the "kindling of a flame." Learning is the calling of a lifetime and a legacy passed on to future generations.

In American higher education, we have for more than a century assigned a major portion of this noble incendiary mission to what we call "general" education. We now make that claim with increasing confidence. Programs informed by vague assumptions about the importance of "breadth" have given way to programs reflecting far higher and more clearly expressed aspirations. At the College of William & Mary, the aim of general education is "to help students develop critical judgment, imagination, and moral autonomy." Southern Methodist University seeks to educate students "as worthy human beings and as citizens, first, and as teachers, lawyers, ministers, research scientists, businessmen, engineers, and so on, second." Oklahoma State University seeks to provide its students with "general knowledge, skills and attitudes conducive to lifelong learning in a complex society." And Loyola University Maryland "challenges" its students "to develop their interests, intellects, outlooks, beliefs, and values."

Strong programs begin with impressive goals. But there is also evidence that what general education programs accomplish for students often falls short of institutional aspirations. Responding to concerns about this gap, the academy has moved to define expectations more clearly and to frame strategies for assessing their accomplishment. The publication in 1994 of the Association of American Colleges and Universities' *Strong Foundations: Twelve Principles for Effective General Education Programs* offered an influential overview of this movement. The book described twelve principles that effective general education programs embody, and, by so doing, offered a rubric against which programs might be measured and through which programs might be improved.

What has happened since 1994 prompts a fresh perspective. In little more than fifteen years, a clear and detailed statement regarding liberal learning outcomes has emerged, and the role of general education in contributing to such outcomes has become more clearly understood. Assessment, prompted initially by external expectations of greater accountability, has become a key tool in programmatic improvement. An epochal paradigm shift from focusing on what is taught to focusing on what is learned can be observed in course syllabi, in statements of departmental outcomes, in revised accreditation standards, in criteria for the evaluation of faculty, and in textbooks. Technology has challenged practice and supported improvement. And the necessity that all the disciplines contribute to the offering of a liberal education to all students has become an ever more widely shared assumption.

Supported and prompted by the progress on these broad fronts within the academy, many institutions have since 1994 taken up the challenge of general education reform and, to a far greater extent than in the past, many have succeeded in achieving genuine progress. As a result, there has developed an instructive community of praxis complementing and in many instances advancing our understanding.

In sum, higher education has become—and continues to become—more intentional with respect to the ends and means of general education and more strategic in its pursuit of those ends through innovative means. In the tradition of *Strong Foundations,* this fresh overview seeks both to celebrate that progress and, in so doing, to further it.

—Paul L. Gaston

Acknowledgments

General Education and Liberal Learning embodies robust collaboration. The current attention to general education and the role it plays in undergraduate education provided the catalyst for this new volume, but the contributors sought also to build on the earlier AAC&U Project on Strong Foundations in General Education and the subsequent publication of *Strong Foundations: Twelve Principles for Effective General Education Programs*. Hence the director of that project, Jerry Gaff, and the chief synthesizer of that publication, Karen Maitland Schilling, agreed to provide guidance for this new publication. Ann Ferren, who served on the original project's advisory board, also agreed to contribute to the continuity of themes and principles for effective general education programs. Two community college leaders, J. Elizabeth Clark and Dwight Smith, brought much-needed insight and expertise on educational aims and outcomes from the sector of higher education where half of American students begin their postsecondary education and often complete much of their general education. Peggy Maki, an international assessment consultant, contributed the national and international perspective on the evidence of student learning that is emerging in support of the effective principles and practices described in this publication. And Barbara Wright offered valuable insights from the arena of regional accreditation associations, which have insisted that campuses pay attention to learning outcomes and assessment of learning for all students through general education programs and majors.

AAC&U's Laura Donnelly-Smith kept this collaborative effort on track and was attentive to a high publication standard. She managed to coordinate the work of the contributors in their far-flung locations both here and in Europe, and ultimately completed the editing of the final manuscript. Darbi Bossman, AAC&U's graphic designer, ably designed the publication. I also wish to thank the campuses that are highlighted in this volume for the continuing work of their faculty and staff in establishing, refining, and sustaining quality general education programs for their students and institutions. Without the work of these exemplars, and the many others we could not mention in these few pages, general education would not make its vibrant and compelling contribution to undergraduate education.

PART ONE: General Education, Liberal Education

Introduction
TERREL L. RHODES

The Association of American Colleges and Universities' seminal work on general education, *Strong Foundations: Twelve Principles for Effective General Education Programs*, opened with the following observation:

> A broad general education for undergraduate students is an ideal that has guided American colleges and universities since their inception. The earliest colleges offered a uniform classical education, and that tradition continued until the late nineteenth and early twentieth centuries. The growth of science, the expansion and subdivision of knowledge, the development of academic disciplines, and the need for specialized workers—these and other factors cracked the uniformity and gave rise to depth of study in a specialization as a different ideal. Since then, the ideals of breadth and depth, together, have been regarded as the defining elements of quality in baccalaureate education. (Association of American Colleges 1994, i)

That volume was written at a time of renewed interest in general education and its importance in preparing students for success. It grew from such earlier Association of American Colleges[1] works as *Integrity in the College Curriculum* (1985) and *A New Vitality in General Education* (1988). The group that prepared *Strong Foundations* was charged with identifying critical factors for sustaining effective general education programs regardless of the type of higher education institution providing the program. Several national educational leaders and a set of representatives from seventeen diverse campuses combined their experience in general education reform and identified twelve principles for successful general education programs.

Much has happened during the fifteen years since *Strong Foundations* was published. This current volume reinforces the earlier principles that were identified as promoting effective general education programs, but also incorporates newer practices that have emerged in the intervening years. *General Education and Liberal Learning: Principles of Effective Practice* comes at a time when general education again is receiving renewed attention. General education is also under attack as campuses struggle with economic stress and policy demands for more students to be educated more quickly. Several states,

TERREL L. RHODES *is vice president for quality, curriculum, and assessment at the Association of American Colleges and Universities.*

---
1 The Association of American Colleges became the Association of American Colleges and Universities in 1995.

including New York, have entered into discussions on encouraging more high school students to begin taking college courses after the tenth grade, long before they graduate from high school (Dillon 2010). Others are exploring ways to reduce the credit hours required for associate and baccalaureate degree programs by reducing required general education credits.

At the same time, we find chief academic officers reflecting the renewed interest in and attention to general education among their faculties. In a recent survey of AAC&U member institutions, 56 percent of chief academic officers reported that their campuses are devoting more attention to general education than they did five years ago. Only 3 percent indicated that they were devoting less attention to general education programs (Hart Research Associates 2009, 1). And while four in five campuses continue to rely upon the "breadth and depth" tradition for general education, most campuses have modified the distribution model with more recent innovations, such as learning communities, common intellectual experiences, thematic courses, upper-division requirements, and undergraduate research. In addition, seventy-eight percent of institutions have a common set of learning outcomes in place, and two-thirds of campuses, including those that use modified distribution models, report that they have adopted "clear learning goals" for their general education programs (Hart Research Associates 2009, 8–9). Of those institutions with common outcomes, large percentages identify a range of specific areas of knowledge and skill as part of their outcome lists (see fig. 1).

The newer pedagogies and practices being incorporated into general education programs across the country not only reflect what faculty and other academic profes-

Figure 1: Areas of Knowledge/Intellectual Skill Addressed by Common Learning Outcomes

Proportion of institutions with campuswide outcomes saying their set of common learning goals addresses each area of knowledge.

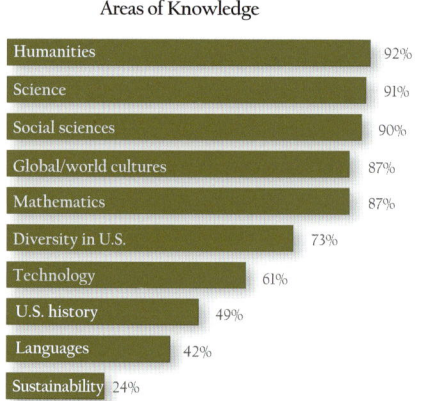

Source: Hart Research Associates 2009

sionals report as important foci for teaching and learning, but also represent an emerging consensus among employers who report on what they seek in college graduates. The educational outcomes that initially were viewed as innovative markers of undergraduate education when they appeared in *Greater Expectations: A New Vision for Learning as a Nation Goes to College* (Association of American Colleges and Universities 2002), and then later in the expanded argument articulating the essential learning outcomes and Principles of Excellence in *College Learning for the New Global Century* (Association of American Colleges and Universities 2007), have become the framework for learning in all types of two- and four-year institutions.

Employers echo the call for more emphasis on college learning outcomes. In a recent national survey conducted for AAC&U, employers indicated that two- and four-year colleges should be placing more emphasis on several key learning outcomes to increase graduates' potential to be successful, contributing members of today's global society (Hart Research Associates 2010). The learning aims and outcomes that employers perceive to be in need of increased focus on college campuses range from communication skills to critical thinking and complex problem solving to ethical decision making to scientific literacy and the real-world application of knowledge and skills. Of the seventeen learning outcomes tested in the survey, a majority of employers think that colleges should place more emphasis on fifteen of them. For eight of these learning outcomes, fully 70 percent or more of employers think that colleges should place more emphasis on them.

The areas in which employers feel that colleges most need to increase their focus include (1) written and oral communication, (2) critical thinking and analytical reasoning, (3) the application of knowledge and skills in real-world settings, (4) complex problem solving and analysis, (5) ethical decision making, (6) teamwork skills, (7) innovation and creativity, and (8) concepts and developments in science and technology (Hart Research Associates 2010, 9).

The demand for better-prepared graduates with broader and higher-level skills and abilities is not directed solely to the elite liberal arts colleges or top research universities. Anthony Carnevale at Georgetown University's Center for Education and the Workforce said that, "irrespective of college major or institutional selectivity, what matters to career success is students' development of a broad set of cross-cutting capacities…" (Carnevale and Humphreys 2010). Even though employees' real earnings have declined in the past few years, the earnings advantage of a college degree persists basically unchanged when compared to individuals with a high school diploma or with no secondary education credential. Future job growth promises to increase this trend, since more of the new jobs projected for the coming decades will require postsecondary levels of knowledge and abilities. Carnevale finds that the more skills and abilities that are required by the job—reflecting the types of learning outcomes associated with effective general education programs—the higher the average earnings. Across the board, job category notwithstanding, the higher the level of liberal learning required by a job, the higher the earnings (Center for Education and the Workforce 2009).

At the same time, policy makers in this country are exploring ways to accelerate completion of college degrees by shortening the time and credits required for completion. They are paying attention to the Bologna Process in Europe and often referencing the three-year baccalaureate provided in some other countries. Yet many countries around the world are increasingly looking at the American model of general education (Gaston 2010). In most of the world, postsecondary educational systems have historically focused on the major with no general education component, thus allowing students to complete a baccalaureate degree in three years. The global equivalent of general education was considered something to be accomplished prior to postsecondary education. In addition, international tests of student knowledge—like the Programme for International Student Assessment exams—are pointed to as evidence for the European approach, because the results have continued to rank European and Asian students ahead of American students.

At the same time that many in the United States are encouraging higher education to emulate existing European models, numerous international educators express the opinion that American graduates seem to be more innovative than their own students, more able to transfer knowledge across disciplinary and conceptual boundaries, and more adept at applying their knowledge to unscripted problems and situations. Each year, the AAC&U office and AAC&U member campuses are visited by delegations from places like the Netherlands, Japan, Taiwan, Hong Kong, and Bulgaria, all of whom want to learn more about the American system of higher education. In particular, they express their belief that the combination of general education with the major is the underlying "secret" of the innovation and creativity that they see in graduates of American colleges and universities—not just in American students, but in their own students who study in the United States and return to their home countries. It is fascinating that just as some policy makers and educators in this country are exploring ways to reduce general education because they wish to mimic the success of European education, or because of cost savings, much of the rest of the world is exploring how to incorporate general education into its higher education systems. Indeed, Japan and Hong Kong recently have adopted general education outcomes and requirements for their baccalaureate systems. China is sending leadership teams from its top tier universities to the United States to learn how to incorporate general education and "liberal arts" emphases in its own university curricula.

The conversation about the effectiveness of general education partly revolves around the evidence supporting the value of general education learning. The twelfth principle identified in *Strong Foundations*—effective assessment of learning outcomes—has become one of the driving forces in evaluating and improving student achievement and in more effectively communicating findings to both campus and external audiences. Faculty, accreditors, policy makers, and students are demanding to see evidence of student learning. The good news is that evidence of student learning is beginning to be accumulated and communicated.

One of the most widely recognized studies on student outcomes and the impact of pedagogies and practices on student learning is the National Survey of Student Engagement (NSSE), originated by George Kuh and now directed by Alexander C. McCormick. The large number of institutions using the NSSE and the number of years that response data have been collected have allowed correlations to be made among the practices and pedagogies used in the curricula and the reported gains on measures of student success. In brief, students who have participate in what AAC&U has called "high-impact practices" (HIPs)—including undergraduate research, first-year experiences, learning communities, internships and community-based learning experiences, study abroad, and capstone courses—exhibit higher rates of retention and earn higher grade point averages than students who report less or no participation in HIPs. In particular, students who report early and multiple participation in HIPs are more engaged in their learning—especially the students who come to college least prepared for postsecondary education (Kuh 2008).

Blaich and Wise (2009) at the Wabash College Center of Inquiry found in their national study of the first college year that some of these same practices—i.e., learning communities, applied learning, and team projects—make a difference in students' learning outcomes, but that few students have the opportunity in their first year of college to participate in or experience these practices. Even though the study found little growth among college freshmen on many of the essential learning outcomes, the evidence suggests that when students do experience the practices, there is growth and learning as a result.

These findings support the need to incorporate the types of practices and principles associated with effective general education programs identified in this volume into any campus's programmatic structure. Incorporation of these practices and principles into a campus's entire curriculum and cocurriculum would appear to support enhanced student learning. Indeed, the often-heard assumption that most of the broad learning aims and outcomes students need to attain are the sole purview of general education is rapidly disappearing. The essential learning our students need must be pervasive in general education, but the same set of skills and abilities must be more deeply embedded throughout the curriculum and cocurriculum, becoming more sophisticated, complex, and challenging as students move through major programmatic study. The underlying approach to general education learning reflected in the inoculation model of the last century—if students need to write, take a writing course; if students need ethical reasoning, take a philosophy course; if students need global understanding, take a course with an international focus—is no longer adequate. The research on cognitive development, deep learning, and mastery supports the value of intentional approaches to learning that are iterative, recurring, incremental, and progressively more challenging as students move through their educational careers. There are benefits to approaches that provide students with multiple opportunities to apply their learning to new, unscripted problems, and that are scaffolded in ways that allow students to develop their skills and abilities in intentional ways.

Particularly in general education, modern undergraduate education necessitates new ways to think about and organize our approaches to teaching and learning. No longer do nearly all students begin their undergraduate education immediately following graduation from high school. No longer do students attend a single college from their first to senior years. The majority attend more than one postsecondary institution during their college careers. Many attend multiple institutions at the same time when they live in a region where multiple institutions are within close proximity. As technology allows for online courses and programs, students living anywhere often can avail themselves of courses from colleges and universities around the globe while attending a local institution at the same time.

Because general education programs typically contain the courses that are most likely to be offered by all institutions or online, the challenge becomes one of organizing undergraduate liberal learning in a manner that recognizes student attendance patterns and allows for learning to be engaged and facilitated across the multitude of course names, numbers, and locations representing the array of methods by which students enroll. Campuses across the country are responding with the adoption of learning outcomes, exemplified by AAC&U's Liberal Education and America's Promise (LEAP) initiative, and the articulation of shared expectations for what student learning should look like for these outcomes as students progress through their careers (Rhodes 2010). AAC&U's Valid Assessment of Learning in Undergraduate Education (VALUE) project has worked with campuses nationwide to develop fifteen rubrics, each focusing on one learning outcome, that can be adapted to meet institutional assessment needs. The focus for judging student learning is shifting from the simple listing of courses and credits on a transcript to recording, reporting, and demonstrating learning through the work our students do in their classes and related activities—often organized within electronic portfolios that can be carried from campus to campus throughout a student's career. In this way, learning can be recognized wherever it occurs, regardless of the formal boundaries that may separate the locus for learning.

The current volume, *General Education and Liberal Learning*, picks up on the work of *Strong Foundations* on the principles of effective general education programs, incorporates the research and expertise developed during the intervening fifteen years, and renews the commitment to the intentional institutional practices, pedagogies, and principles that are associated with effective general education in the twenty-first century. The contributors have created a bold and vibrant framework within which individuals and campuses can examine their current general education programs and envision new ways to achieve enhanced student learning through the organization and implementation of this most important and foundational component of undergraduate liberal learning: general education.

Chapter 1
Imperatives for and Drivers of Change
Paul L. Gaston

Although an institution's general education program cannot by itself ensure that students receive all the outcomes of a liberal education, a commitment to liberal education requires the support that only an effective general education program can offer.

What the well-educated college graduate should know and be able to do develops within several environments. One is the curriculum, which should include a strong general education offering, study in the major that reinforces the aims of general education, and a judicious selection of electives. Another is the cocurriculum. The opportunities found there for community engagement, student work, and campus leadership can offer a powerful contribution. Beyond the curriculum altogether, campus life and recreation, student housing, and social life may enhance the overall educational experience. A former president of James Madison University once observed that even campus maintenance and landscaping should convey a respect for scholarship (R.E. Carrier, pers. comm.). Whether in the Ivy League, community colleges, public comprehensive universities, or private liberal arts colleges, liberal education at its most substantive reflects a spectrum of learning and experience.

This overview of general education and liberal learning focuses on but one part of the matrix that leads to a college education—but it is a critical part. By acknowledging the liberal education goals of higher education and examining carefully the ways in which effective general education can further such goals, we can clarify principles that may assist colleges and universities in strengthening general education and thus assuring more effective liberal education.

As suggested in the introduction, the first prompt for this publication lies in a 1994 publication by the Association of American Colleges, *Strong Foundations,* a cogent and substantive platform for conceiving, planning, and implementing more effective general education programs. The slim volume draws on both informed reflection and awareness of exemplary practice in presenting "twelve principles for effective general education programs" (AAC 1994). The publication proved both prescient and influential. Many of the principles it set forth remain relevant and compelling today, and they are evident on campuses where there is improvement in programs of general education.

The second prompt was Greater Expectations, a major initiative the Association of American Colleges and Universities conducted between 2000 and 2006, which articulated the aims and purposes of a twenty-first century liberal education, identified innovative models that improve campus practices and learning for all undergraduate students, and advocated for a comprehensive approach to reform. The work of the Greater Expectations initiative laid the foundation for AAC&U's current initiative, Liberal Education and America's Promise (LEAP). In 2007, the LEAP national report, *College Learning for the New Global Century,* was published. The LEAP report provides the third prompt: a clearly structured statement outlining the essential learning outcomes of a college education (see fig. 2). Many colleges and universities have found in this statement a convenient point of departure for discussions regarding the baccalaureate and the vital contribution of general education in offering all students the benefits of a liberal education. Incorporating many years of deliberation and drawing on a wide range of authorities and good practices, the essential learning outcomes represent nothing less than the first widely accepted statement within the academy of what students should know and be able to do when they graduate from a baccalaureate program embodying effective general education (AAC&U 2007, 12).

The three prompts for this overview are closely related. Writing in *Strong Foundations,* Jerry Gaff cited a "heuristic" definition of general education: "the knowledge, skills, and attitudes that all of us use and live by during most of our lives" (AAC 1994, ii). No one would argue with the continuing relevance of these elements as touchstones for effective general education and as assumptions behind an institution's more inclusive liberal education aims. It seems fitting therefore that the essential learning outcomes AAC&U promotes through LEAP stand on "strong foundations" first set forth in 1994 and now organized more broadly into critical domains of knowledge, as follows:
- knowledge of human cultures and the physical and natural world
- intellectual and practical skills
- personal and social responsibility
- integrative and applied learning

The essential learning outcomes are ideally adapted to the changing environment of higher education and represent a platform on which strategic programmatic reform can be built. But the outcomes also represent an important element in the environment, a strong influence on many of the changes taking place within it, and, as suggested above, a prompt for considering both the attributes of a comprehensive commitment to liberal education and the crucial role of general education within that commitment. Hence, in contrast with the observers in Robert Frost's enigmatic poem "Neither Out Far Nor In Deep," *General Education and Liberal Learning* will both "look out far," so as to acknowledge the circumstances emphasizing the importance of offering a liberal education to all students, and "look in deep" at how our understanding of effective general education, so vital to our overall liberal education commitment, is becoming richer, more substantive, and, in an important sense, more ambitious.

Why do we seek this broader vision now? Important changes in the environment of higher education have typically emerged gradually over time—lots of time. But increasingly, higher education is experiencing disruptive rather than gradual forms of change. Trends glimpsed in *Strong Foundations* have accelerated. Other trends of emerging significance have become increasingly influential. And efforts to respond to these trends through an evolving vision of how general education contributes to overall educational goals have produced a strong record of innovation. In order to understand more fully why the new century calls for a fresh vision of essential learning and to appreciate what has been achieved in pursuit of that vision, we should acknowledge some of these trends and consider their relevance for general education.

Figure 2: Essential Learning Outcomes

Beginning in school, and continuing at successively higher levels across their college studies, students should prepare for twenty-first-century challenges by gaining:

Knowledge of Human Cultures and the Physical and Natural World
- Through study in the sciences and mathematics, social sciences, humanities, histories, languages, and the arts

Focused by engagement with big questions, both contemporary and enduring

Intellectual and Practical Skills, including
- Inquiry and analysis
- Critical and creative thinking
- Written and oral communication
- Quantitative literacy
- Information literacy
- Teamwork and problem solving

Practiced extensively, across the curriculum, in the context of progressively more challenging problems, projects, and standards for performance

Personal and Social Responsibility, including
- Civic knowledge and engagement—local and global
- Intercultural knowledge and competence
- Ethical reasoning and action
- Foundations and skills for lifelong learning

Anchored through active involvement with diverse communities and real-world challenges

Integrative and Applied Learning, including
- Synthesis and advanced accomplishment across general and specialized studies

Demonstrated through the application of knowledge, skills, and responsibilities to new settings and complex problems

Source: AAC&U 2007, 12

The World Is Demanding More

As noted above, an effective general education program—whether in the form of a coherent program or explicit, actionable expectations requiring intentional, systematic response—cannot do it all. But the contributions general education makes have come to be recognized as particularly relevant to the demands of a new century. A strong general education program provides the skills, traits, and awareness that support not only strong beginnings in the worlds of employment and service, but also the capacity for growth that characterizes agile thinkers, enthusiastic learners, and effective team members.

As expectations of college graduates have evolved, the demands made of general education have necessarily developed as well. While effective programs of general education should contribute significantly to all the broad domains of knowledge set forth in *College Learning for the New Global Century,* such programs above all ensure that students experience the ways of knowing that must not only be grasped but "practiced extensively, across the curriculum, in the context of progressively more challenging problems, projects, and standards for performance" (AAC&U 2007, 12). These include inquiry and analysis, critical and creative thinking, written and oral communication, quantitative literacy, information literacy, teamwork, and problem solving.

Such ways of knowing have always been important, but the demands of the new century have expressed a singular urgency. Never before has there been so great a need for learned and adaptable citizens capable of taking apart and understanding complex problems, of identifying reliability and authority among the many sources of information, of appreciating the quantitative realities that may lie beneath the surface, of thinking creatively about solutions, of communicating *to* others the emerging results of their work, and of working *with* others to bring solutions to practice. In short, what general education can offer is what all students need to live in a complex global society.

This sense of urgency is well captured in the recent revision of general education at the University of Nebraska–Lincoln (UNL). "Achievement-Centered Education" seeks to offer students opportunities "to develop and to apply relevant skills, knowledge, and social responsibilities no matter what their majors or career aspirations are." Each of these components is articulated through direct, active, assessable imperatives. For instance, instead of offering a vague aspiration that students learn to write well, UNL expresses the commitment that its students will "write texts, in various forms, with an identified purpose, that respond to specific audience needs, incorporate research or existing knowledge, and use applicable documentation and appropriate conventions of format or structure." To further the opportunities offered for arts awareness, UNL asserts that its students will "use knowledge, theories, or methods appropriate to the arts to understand their context and significance." And rather than floating the hopeful expectation that students will somehow find it possible to integrate their experiences in different realms of knowledge, UNL calls on students to "generate a creative or scholarly product that requires broad knowledge, appropriate technical proficiency, information collection, synthesis, interpretation, presentation, and reflection" (University of Nebraska–Lincoln 2008).

> *Never before has there been so great a need for learned and adaptable citizens capable of taking apart and understanding complex problems.*

A Different Student Body

Beneath many earnest twentieth-century statements of general education goals lie two unstated premises: most students will be able to devote their full attention to their college experience, and most will complete their general education at the institution from which they will graduate. This vision continues to inform many goals statements, but for many institutions and students, the reality is now very different. As of 2007, according to the National Center for Education Statistics, "about 46 percent of full-time and 81 percent of part-time college students ages 16–24 were employed" (U.S. Department of Education 2009).

Students now for the most part study part time while balancing their educational goals with the necessity of employment. And many part-time students are *full-time* workers. While the percentage of college students who work has increased incrementally, the percentage of students who work full time while attending college has risen sharply, from 5.6 percent in 1985 to 10.4 percent as of 2000 (Orszag, Orszag, and Whitmore 2001), and up to 32.2 percent in 2007–8 (U.S. Department of Education 2008). Those who follow these trends closely now differentiate between "students who work" and "workers who study." Students are increasingly mobile as well, moving from one institution to another as their needs and locations dictate. As of 2006, 17 percent of undergraduate students transferred from one institution to another at least one time, and 2 percent transferred two or three times (U.S. Department of Education 2007). These percentages would be even higher if students who coenrolled in more than one institution at a time were included.

If the academy is to meet its goal of providing the benefits of essential education to all students, it must take seriously these demographic and cultural shifts. This is especially important as institutions strive to increase access to higher education and work to help students complete the baccalaureate. One of the important principles set forth in *Strong Foundations* is that a college or university must reach clarity on what its graduates should know and be able to do. Only in that broader context of preparation for careers and lifelong learning can the specific goals for general education make sense. But if fewer than half of an institution's graduates receive their general education at the institution from which they receive the baccalaureate degree, what can an institution do to ensure that all its graduates meet its liberal learning goals?

Diversity as a Critical Educational Value

Only within the last fifteen years has substantive research, acknowledging widely accepted moral and cultural values, confirmed the ways in which a diverse learning environment supports effective education. Classrooms with a variety of student and faculty perspectives in play, supported by a rich multiplicity of content and materials, are dynamic and engaging. As a result, increasing access to education and diversifying the faculty remain not only urgent social imperatives, but also have emerged as pedagogical necessities. In addition, the pursuit of diversity in the curriculum has encouraged a more inclusive understanding of essential learning itself. As curricular choices have multiplied, a broader opportunity to develop distinctive approaches to global understanding, cross-cultural competence, and social responsibility has emphasized the importance of thoughtful choices in curricular design to promote essential learning.

A 1995 AAC&U study, *Diversity in Higher Education*, still offers a useful point of departure for an appreciation of this force within the "new environment." Diversity must become, in a word, "transformative" (Musil 1995, 62). But the emphasis of the 1995 study on social change, while entirely appropriate to and necessary for the circumstances it documents, suggests also a process of growth within this imperative. Early experience with "diversity courses" has expanded to include consideration of the curriculum as a whole and of how it is offered within an enabling environment. A more recent study by Hu and Kuh concludes that students who enjoy the benefits of a diverse learning environment regard those benefits as directly related to their *educational* gains (Hu and Kuh 2003).

Economic Pressures

Issues of funding have had a measurable impact on both college students and their institutions in the twenty-first century, and anyone concerned with strengthening general education must take such issues into account. Reductions in state support for public institutions, even before the recession that emerged in 2007, prompted many institutions to increase class sizes, rely more on part-time faculty, and measure any innovation in terms of cost effectiveness. Private institutions have not been immune from such pressures and have had to make difficult choices among such concerns as financial aid, enhanced technology, and faculty salaries. Reductions in the value of endowments and economic pressures to constrain tuition have exerted similar pressures. In this environment, preserving funding for faculty development, small seminars, team teaching, and undergraduate research, for example, requires that a strong case be made by faculty.

In turn, students and families faced with tuition increases that have outstripped annual increases in the cost of living have become far more pragmatic and urgent about why they are seeking higher education. Professional programs that appear to promise more immediate job placement have great appeal. In this environment, general education can be vulnerable. To students who must work long hours to pay tuition, any requirements that appear unrelated or tangential to their vocational ambitions may appear simply as impediments.

However, as we acknowledge the economic forces that bear on students, teachers, and the curriculum itself, we must respond to them appropriately and avoid injudicious, counter-productive concessions. Agreement on principles of effective general education—and, more broadly, on overarching liberal education goals—should lead us to articulate more forcefully the connections between general education and success in a turbulent global economy. Strong general education programs enable students to prepare for and adapt to uncertainty, to recognize and respond to emerging opportunities, and to exercise creativity when others are hunkering down.

Of course, economic challenges can promote positive innovations aimed at efficiency and effectiveness, such as the use of course-management systems and electronic library resources. In some institutions, budget constraints have prompted a fresh clarity

Strong general education programs enable students to prepare for and adapt to uncertainty.

as to priorities, a return of the focus to student learning and away from less essential operations. And many students balancing work and study do understand the contribution general education makes to providing them with the skills and capacities that employers value.

The bottom line of this balance sheet is clear. Periods of economic uncertainty cast into even higher relief the values of liberal learning. Those who pay attention to such values will identify opportunities for investment—not retrenchment.

The Influence of Technology

When *Strong Foundations* was published, the "technology" of choice for instruction was the overhead projector. Computers were already in wide use, of course, but the potential influence of the Internet was only beginning to emerge. Not until 2000 would Blackboard, Inc., file its patent for "Internet-based education support systems and methods." Wikipedia, now the world's largest (if perhaps least reliable) encyclopedia, was founded in 2001. Google searches began less than a decade ago. And the availability of such services through standard wireless transmission protocols? Also a twenty-first-century phenomenon—and one that spans the globe, linking students and faculty members not only to important data but also to one another.

The significance for learning through these remarkable developments is conspicuous. Faculty members now routinely support their lectures with projected computer slides and other visual materials appropriate to varied learning styles. Courseware systems enable faculty members and students to further the work of the classroom through informal discussion, through prompts to additional reading, and through opportunities for out-of-class collaborative work. Classroom response mechanisms, e.g., "clickers," offer strategies for ensuring some degree of student participation even in very large course sections. Faculty can even connect their students and courses with classrooms abroad to promote international perspectives without the costs of travel. And electronic portfolios provide a new learning and assessment tool.

But there is also a sense in which technology, specifically the Internet, poses a critical epistemological issue for general education. When the invention of printing led in time to a proliferation of presses and publications, scholars faced the new challenge of enabling their students to discriminate between authoritative and unreliable texts. Now a similar challenge has arisen, as students must be able to understand and apply criteria for determining the validity and objectivity of sources from reliable, somewhat reliable, and deeply unreliable providers. Faculty must caution their students against uncritical reliance on Web resources such as Wikipedia, urge that scholarly research utilize methods beyond Google, and work with the library staff to teach information literacy.

Perhaps the greatest challenge is distance learning. Should general education courses be offered online, thereby foregoing the intangible benefits of classroom collegiality in favor of student convenience and remunerative enrollments? As faculty experiment with this new format, many have learned how to preserve the value of discussion, immediate feedback, and coaching. At the same time, both faculty and students concede that face-to-face learning has benefits. Thus, many campuses are striving for a mixed model of delivery.

The Assessment Imperative

In 1994 it would have been difficult to visualize how influential and pervasive the assessment of educational outcomes would become. The issue is no longer one primarily of accountability—even though such expectations continue to emerge. Rather, the principal value of assessment lies within a larger picture, as a complement to the learning outcomes that give purpose and design to general education.

Because we will attend to assessment as an "effective practice" in part 3, and will do so at some length, it may be enough to note here the positive influence assessment has had within higher education. Properly conceived and implemented, assessment provides a productive focus on overriding questions of priority, for example:

- What should students learn and be able to do?
- How can we measure most usefully the effectiveness of programs and institutions in assisting students to their respective educational gains?
- What can such measures reveal to those who support student learning—faculty members, librarians, cocurricular leaders, administrators, and many others—so that they can do so more effectively?

To be sure, a heavy-handed autocratic effort to implement an assessment program in pursuit of poorly understood institutional concerns can arouse resistance. Undertakings that confuse the evaluative potential of assessment with its potential for supporting institutional strengthening may also run aground. Precisely because assessment, properly considered, drives to the heart of teaching and learning, its adaptation to institutional needs must be managed with sensitivity and vision.

Some commentators describe an "accountability loop"—a useful phrase if accountability is not seen solely as a means of attesting to compliance with minimal standards of adequacy. If accountability is seen rather as a means by which an institution remains accountable to itself, to its goals for student learning and the expansion of knowledge, then assessment stands as a lynchpin in a continuing loop of quality improvement and as an emblem of the academy's fresh commitment to examining, understanding, and increasing its effectiveness.

The Changing Roles of and Pressures on Faculty

Early reviews of the quality of general education programs focused primarily on the faculty who taught the courses in those programs. More recently, such reviews have led to concerns about the efficacy of a program that stands alone. Education cannot take the form of a single inoculation; it requires incremental "booster shots." Early exposure to important ideas, skills, and values is critical, but repeated exposure provides important reinforcement and increasing sophistication. Recent efforts to "connect" general education with the major, important in themselves, have thus yielded an important insight: all members of the faculty share a responsibility for their students' liberal learning, and all have an impact. Whether their disciplines are accounting, history, or nursing, faculty members at all levels of the curriculum can provide reinforcement and practice for their students' pursuit of liberal learning outcomes.

Engaging faculty in sharing responsibility for essential outcomes is not easy. Indeed, a faculty member whose dedication to a particular discipline admits no acknowledgment of a shared responsibility for liberal learning may undermine the broad learning goals to which an institution is committed. Faculty development may not persuade all faculty to take an active interest in general education, but can be effective in helping faculty appreciate the role general education plays in support of the major outcomes. In part 4, when we discuss how the benefits of effective general education may be sustained, we will consider the role of faculty across the institution in more detail, but for the present it belongs in this review of environmental changes that deserve our recognition.

The New Learning Environment

This survey of changing elements within the environment of higher education has covered considerable ground within a short space. An influential new consensus on educational outcomes, shifting demographics within the student body, an increasing appreciation for the educational importance of diversity, pressures arising from declines in funding, the influence of technology, the considerable expansion of the influence of assessment, and a growing recognition that the faculty and curriculum as a whole must help to provide the benefits of a liberal education—these influences taken together represent a positive environmental shift of seismic proportions.

Yet there are other environmental elements that might have been examined as well. Some, such as the desirable erosion of boundaries between academic offerings and student life, are mentioned below in the discussion of important principles. Others, such as the influence of new approaches to institutional accounting that may impose increased "productivity" demands on general education, must await another venue. But what seems abundantly clear even from this overview is that higher education—and general education in particular—must adapt in responsible and creative ways to a changed environment. And that is why clarity about the strengths identified with strong general education programs is critical.

PART TWO: General Education as Curricular Cornerstone

Chapter 2
Principles of Strong General Education Programs
PAUL L. GASTON

General education programs that contribute significantly to liberal education outcomes embody several principles. Programs that fall short can be strengthened by colleagues who observe and pursue such principles. In this chapter, we define such principles by paying attention to characteristics common to strong programs.

While strong general education programs may be highly distinctive in some ways, they tend also to express broadly shared principles of good practice. Whether undertaken as a road trip or as an Internet voyage, a tour of widely admired and often-referenced programs can reveal such principles and suggest a kind of measuring rod, or *kanon*, which may be useful to others. This chapter attends to five of the most important of the factors that appear to support programmatic effectiveness.

First, strong programs embody and express a clear vision for general education, one grounded in an institutional commitment to the benefits of a liberal education for all students. Second, strong programs benefit from broad understanding within the college or university of the important roles played in general education by all institutional constituencies. Third, strong programs can present evidence at every curricular level of a concern with effective pedagogy that expresses the purposeful pursuit of explicitly stated learning objectives. Fourth, strong programs demonstrate appreciation for the role of the cocurriculum in enhancing and sustaining the gains achieved in the classroom. Finally, strong programs require and express strong leadership from many levels.

Clarity of Vision

In calling for a commitment to make explicit "the *point* of general education," *Strong Foundations* established a fundamental principle. An effective general education program not only conveys its "point" but explains why and how its particular priorities have been chosen, how the different elements in the program correspond to these priorities, and how its structure reflects those priorities. Ideally, a student should understand how every

NORTH CAROLINA STATE UNIVERSITY

RALEIGH, NORTH CAROLINA

Looking Inward to Improve Intentionality

At North Carolina State, reforming the general education program meant looking inward first: administrators acknowledged that the categories of offerings within the general education program, the objectives of the categories, and the justification for courses within the categories were all unclear. As a result, the new program, implemented in the summer of 2009, sets explicit expectations for students, and details how they will integrate different academic disciplines through an interdisciplinary study requirement.

UNITED STATES MILITARY ACADEMY

WEST POINT, NEW YORK

An Interdisciplinary Core

At West Point, students complete a thirty-course general education core that constitutes almost 75 percent of their academic experience. While core requirements of this size are unusual at liberal arts colleges, one of West Point's main academic goals for students is that they become self-directed learners capable of applying knowledge to new situations. The core courses are highly interdisciplinary and include a special focus on integrating foreign language with history and global studies.

---

class meeting contributes to the learning goals of every course and how course goals are related to programmatic goals.

Sound programs do not emerge by happenstance. They express the deliberate pursuit of a design aimed at that institution's vision of a well-educated graduate. For instance, if an aim of the program is that students "unify and bring together their learning across courses, over time, and between curricular and cocurricular experiences," as at the University of Wisconsin–Eau Claire, the structure of the program must guide students accordingly so as to ensure that such integration routinely takes place. Similarly, programs that emphasize learning in depth must direct students into opportunities for recursive learning. If the program promises that students will develop a sense of civic responsibility, it should lead students into appropriate activities, reflection, and evaluation. Because no general education program can do everything, strong programs necessarily embody difficult choices among many appealing and worthy objectives. And they explain the choices that have been made to students and to the broader community.

That this most basic challenge remains to be fulfilled on many campuses appears both in musings within institutions and from nationwide surveys. In fact, many campuses begin their reform efforts when they became aware of unfulfilled expectations. The process of general education reform at North Carolina State began with some candid admissions: the categories of offerings within the program, the objectives of the categories, and the justification for courses within the categories were "unclear" (Bresciani and Anderson n.d.). Thus, the new program implemented in the summer of 2009 has clear objectives and offers the means to accomplish them. A commitment that students learn to integrate different disciplines now appears in an explicit requirement for interdisciplinary study.

Another institution that has used the reform of general education to promote a clearer understanding of institutional mission is the United State Military Academy at West Point.[2] Consistent with its specialized purpose—the education of officers for the U.S. Army—West Point has refined its focus on liberal education through an expanded core curriculum and an emphasis on curricular integration. Students at West Point complete a thirty-course general education core that constitutes almost 75 percent of their academic experience. While a core of this size is not common among colleges and universities, West Point's mission requires that its students be broadly educated so that they can become self-directed learners capable of applying knowledge to new situations. And since 2005, the academy's focus on integrative learning has led to a linking of history and language courses to promote the deep exploration of global connections. Given plans to integrate more of the academy's thirteen academic departments, the role of integrative learning is likely to become even more characteristic of West Point's mission in the future.

Clarity of vision need not require a change in a program, but may be achieved through renewed commitment and communication with students. Brown University recently revisited

---

2 This and many of the other examples of exemplary practice in general education described in this publication are drawn from feature stories originally published in AAC&U's monthly member publication, *AAC&U News*. The *AAC&U News* archive may be viewed online at www.aacu.org/aacu_news/archives/archive10.cfm.

a curriculum long notable for its lack of specific general education requirements. Working within this tradition, a task force clarified the institution's learning goals with an eye toward ensuring that Brown students become intentional learners with a clear view of what they are trying to accomplish through their studies. One result is a statement, "Liberal Learning at Brown," that defines specific learning goals students are expected to achieve before graduation and suggests ways that students can progress toward these goals—all without mandating specific classes or distribution requirements (Brown Office of the Dean of the College 2008). Other outcomes of the task force's work include recommendations for a more robust advising program and for an e-portfolio requirement that asks students to reflect systematically on their educational choices and the intentions behind them (Donnelly-Smith 2008).

In these and many other institutions, clear awareness of the important role of general education as a curricular cornerstone confers many additional benefits. Students, faculty, and cocurricular directors can find both direction and motivation in a shared conviction. The institution can tell its story more persuasively to potential students, new faculty, and donors. And the ground for continuous improvement and advancement of the institution is solid.

Commitment to Coherence

All too often, general education programs "strive for educational coherence" by foisting onto students the responsibility for achieving it. But as part 3 will explore in more detail, unless the structure of the program and the faculty teaching within it *enable* students to understand the rationale behind the requirements they must satisfy, few students are likely to achieve the objective. After reading through the catalog copy describing general education at his institution, commentator Mark Bauerlein observes that the rhetoric of coherence directed at students may fall on deaf ears. Students are likely to regard an "array" of general education courses "as merely a bunch of random, disconnected courses outside their major . . . a bunch of heterogeneous hoops to pass through" (Bauerlein 2009).

By contrast, Bard College leaves little to chance. Principles of curricular coherence first appear in a three-week intensive introduction to the liberal arts and sciences, are regularly reinforced through a first-year seminar program, and are embedded in the curriculum itself. All first-year students at Bard spend the three weeks prior to the start of fall semester in the Language and Thinking Program, in which small groups of students, under the guidance of faculty members, complete readings, discussions, and writing projects that help them understand the goals and intended outcomes of a Bard education. Students then participate in yearlong first-year seminars that introduce the "important intellectual, cultural, and artistic ideas that serve as a basis for the liberal arts education." In the second year, a program called Moderation requires students to reflect on their educational experience as they move toward in-depth study of their major, and a required senior capstone project ties together four years of learning.

Saint Louis Community College's approach to general education could offer an example of curricular coherence to many institutions. Study toward the associate of arts degree begins with a cornerstone course that introduces principles of college study—including "how to explore ethical choices, understand and argue your own point of view, and understand the argu-

Saint Louis Community College

Saint Louis, Missouri

Sound Preparation for a Four-Year Degree

At all four branches of Saint Louis Community College, students working toward an associate of arts degree begin with a cornerstone course that helps them see the goals of general education and how they fit into the college experience. Then, in addition to skills courses in mathematics and communication, students choose from three categories—arts and humanities, social and behavioral science, and science—to build a forty-two-credit-hour general education program. Students complete their general education experience with a capstone course that includes a final project and prepares them to transfer to a four-year school. Students who complete the entire general education program are assured that their general education credits will be accepted at any Missouri public institution.

> **MICHIGAN STATE UNIVERSITY**
>
> EAST LANSING, MICHIGAN
>
> **Dialogues for Social Responsibility**
>
> Michigan State University (MSU) seeks for its students to understand social responsibility through an approach that will eventually span the full baccalaureate curriculum. In MSU's Twenty-First Century Chautauqua program, based on the example of the historic Chautauqua Institution, students participate in an ongoing series of collaborative campus dialogues on topics like sustainability and human rights. The program, housed within two residential colleges, offers a model for building a culture of responsibility, and catalyzes the development of courses that address the responsibility more broadly.

ments of others." Then, in addition to skills courses in mathematics and communication, students choose from three categories—arts and humanities, social and behavioral science, and science—to build a forty-two-credit-hour program. Students complete their general education experience with a capstone course "that helps bring all the disciplines together" and provides a platform for transfer to a baccalaureate institution (Saint Louis Community College).

Dedication to Educating Responsible Citizens

Colleges and universities that build the baccalaureate curriculum around a strong general education cornerstone typically express a vision of general education that embodies both recognized outcomes and programmatic characteristics that support such outcomes. These outcomes may express different emphases from one institution to another, but increasingly they reflect the developing consensus expressed in the essential learning outcomes as articulated by AAC&U. These need not be further summarized here, but three in particular deserve attention, as they emphasize the importance of a broad institutional commitment to community in many forms. Briefly stated, such principles include an appreciation for the role of general education in fostering a sense of social responsibility, a grasp on important experiential dimensions of learning within and beyond the classroom, and a recognition of the extent to which effective general education may foster a healthier academic community.

Social Responsibility

The discussion of general education through the past fifteen years has moved beyond the assumption that strong "value-based" programs "teach social responsibility" to a more encompassing perspective: students should have the opportunity to develop within and beyond the classroom informed and self-reflective values that emphasize a generous understanding of community and personal responsibility. As suggested in the essential learning outcomes, that understanding should include civic knowledge and engagement—local and global, intercultural knowledge and competence, the capacity for ethical reasoning and action, and a foundation for lifelong learning.

Michigan State University (MSU) seeks to achieve these capacities through an approach that will eventually span the full baccalaureate curriculum. A Carnegie-designated "engaged university," MSU has developed an ongoing series of collaborative campus dialogues based on the example of the historic Chautauqua Institution. The program offers a model for building a culture of responsibility within the residential colleges and has two goals: the exploration of personal, social, and institutional responsibility, and the development of courses that address the larger subject of responsibility itself. Housed within several of MSU's residential colleges, the Chautauqua dialogues bring together small groups of students, faculty members, staff members, and guests for dialogue about a specific topic at regular meetings over the span of a semester. Recent Chautauqua topics have included sustainability and human rights; Martin Luther King Jr., equality, and justice; and creativity, economic development, and ethics. Faculty members are currently using the Chautauqua model to reframe capstone courses already required for undergraduate students by imbedding within them a focus on personal and social responsibility.

Experiential Learning

As *Strong Foundations* proposed, general education programs can "close the gap between lofty program aspirations and their limited role in the formal curriculum" by taking greater advantage of "the extraordinary resources for learning that already exist in the varied activities in the daily lives of students" (AAC 1994). Strong programs do include attention to cocurricular experiences. But to an increasing extent, effective programs offer opportunities for learning that not only complement the curriculum but also are highly intentional, intellectually substantive, closely linked to curricular content, and rich in community engagement.

Among the important advances in cocurricular learning are what can be called "living–learning communities," "residential colleges," or college-based housing. Some programs operate with reference to a first-year-experience program or include freshman interest groups. Some may express a focus on particular disciplines. Others may embody a broad interdisciplinary focus or contribute to campus outreach. In any event, such undertakings serve to blur the distinction between the classroom and campus experiences by providing opportunities for learning in both venues.

As appreciation for the meaning of a "practical" liberal education develops on campuses, many programs make an explicit commitment to engagement and public service in order to turn ideas into action and theory into practice. At Ohio State University, for instance, service learning is defined as "a form of experiential education characterized by student participation in an organized service activity that is connected to specific learning outcomes, meets identified community needs, [and] provides structured time for student reflection and connection of the service experience to learning" (Ohio State University). At Millsaps College in Mississippi, which was named in 2008 and 2009 to the President's Higher Education Community Service Honor Roll, "students recognize that there is more to life than just concentrating on themselves. They are interested in serving others and the College encourages this by linking classes to needs in the community to foster growth through service" (Mississippi Economic Council 2009).

While much of the activity in service learning falls within the disciplines, the implications for general education are striking. At Rhodes College, a commitment to experiential learning, evident in its tradition of community service, has informed implementation of a new general education "Foundations" curriculum. Instead of distribution requirements, the curriculum embodies eleven foundations of liberal learning, one of which is "participation in activities that broaden connections between the classroom and the world" (Rhodes College 2007). This foundation requires that students participate in "outside the gates" experiential learning activities and that they work with faculty to connect these activities to their classroom learning. Making this commitment even more explicit, starting in fall of 2008, Rhodes's "Scholarships to Fellowships" initiative converted all merit scholarships to fellowships with structured out-of-class experiential components.

Finally, there is the technical dimension of out-of-classroom learning. Supportive course delivery software now enables class members to sustain their discussions between class meetings, to collaborate on scholarship, to consult with instructors and one another, and to monitor their performance. Effective general education programs make effective use of such technology to "reach beyond the classroom" at all hours of the day.

RHODES COLLEGE
MEMPHIS, TENNESSEE

Connecting Experience with Classroom Learning

At Rhodes, the general education curriculum is built on eleven "foundations" of liberal learning. One foundation, "participation in activities that broaden connections between the classroom and the world," requires students to complete experiential learning projects within the community and work with faculty members to connect the projects to their classroom learning. In the fall of 2008, the college also transformed all scholarships into fellowships that include structured out-of-class experiential components.

Hostos Community College–City University of New York

Bronx, New York

Highlighting the Relevance of General Education

Hostos Community College declared 2007 the "Year of General Education" and sought, through monthly activities, to emphasize how general education competencies are relevant to all facets of academic and community life. Administrators also seek to ensure that all of the college community's voices—including those of nonacademic staff—are heard. A curricular meeting on preparation for a grant application, open to the entire college community, attracted nonacademic staff including cafeteria workers, electricians, and grounds workers.

Academic Community

The vision set forth in *Strong Foundations* of a stronger sense of community arising from "faculty-student interaction" remains compelling and should remain as a priority. But that priority has grown larger in two respects. First, a more inclusive understanding of the academic community, one that seeks greater consultation and collaboration among all elements within an institution, now includes not only the faculty and students, but also those engaged in student life, in residential services, in university relations, and in campus design. Ensuring productive interchange among students, between students and faculty, and among faculty remains at the heart of this commitment, of course, and an enlarged understanding of how students learn has eroded the familiar distinction between "academic" and "nonacademic."

Second, it has become clear that a sense of academic community rests most securely on a shared commitment to quality and improvement. The 1994 call for programs "consciously designed so that they will continue to evolve" still offers an important reminder that liberal learning and the ways in which it is offered cannot and should not be regarded as fixed, but rather as subject to continuing examination and transformation. And because such examination must reflect the commitment of the college or university as a whole, programs should not only "evolve" but also reflect the clear intent of the academic community in becoming progressively more effective.

The approach of Hostos Community College–City University of New York to general education illustrates an "organic" approach to learning that can strengthen a sense of academic community through the definition of educational outcomes transcending the formal curriculum. Having introduced a new general education curriculum built around learning competencies, the college in 2007 celebrated the "Year of General Education" by exploring questions such as, What does it mean to be human? What is culture and how do we understand it? How do we cross linguistic and cultural borders? A series of minigrants awarded to faculty members prompted pedagogical innovations called "beautiful ideas," intended to refocus existing courses around the school's core learning competencies. Throughout the process, Hostos faculty and administrators have attempted to ensure that voices from all parts of the college—including nonacademic staff—are heard. A recent curricular meeting on preparation for a grant application, open to the entire college community, attracted both faculty members and nonacademic staff including cafeteria workers, electricians, and grounds workers.

In order to sustain the pursuit of "an evolving vision," strong programs measure their progress and reflect upon the results. These important commitments are now viewed as links in a broader recurring cycle supporting qualitative development. There are many interpretations of this cycle, but most embody at least five elements: (1) clear statements of intended learning outcomes associated with the baccalaureate, with the general education program, with the various majors, and with every course in the curriculum; (2) the application of appropriate methods for measuring the extent to which these outcomes are being accomplished; (3) interpretation of the results of such measurements, leading to recommendations for modifications in expectations, structures, or means of delivery; (4) the implementation of such recommendations; and (5) the routine recommencement of the cycle. The object so far as general education is concerned is clear: programs that are increasingly inviting, coherent, and effective. In pursuit of this principle, there is really only one important question: is the general education program becoming progressively stronger? In the shared pursuit of that question lies an important source of academic community.

Appreciation for the Educational Value of the Cocurriculum

Those engaged in effective general education programs understand that faculty members and the learning they support are not solely responsible for its outcomes. They have valuable allies among those who teach in the majors, to be sure, but they have other important allies as well. For many students, vital learning takes place not only in the classroom and library, but also in student organizations, in work–study positions, in residence hall discussions, in intramural athletics, in community engagement—the opportunities to reinforce essential learning outcomes are many. Each of these arenas can be vital to enhancing and sustaining general education outcomes. Residential campuses may have an advantage in promoting engagement, but all types of campuses with both full-time and part-time students are increasingly aware of the role of cocurricular activities in an overall culture of engagement.

It should not be surprising that colleges and universities offering exemplary programs in general education demonstrate proportionate attention to student experiences outside the classroom. In light of an explicit board of trustees commitment to "people, programs and facilities that strengthen academic excellence in each of our schools and colleges," a task force on campus life at Willamette University observes, "we are not well-served if the various college constituencies think in terms of 'academics' vs. social life" (Willamette University 2001). Indeed, says the report, "to the extent that we act as though academic and social life are distinct and even antagonistic spheres, we undercut our efforts to achieve the range of objectives that we have set in educating our students." In response, the campus developed a plan for residential commons complexes, a community of fraternity and sorority houses, and a new student center designed to encourage consistent attentiveness to the institution's educational objectives and how they may best be served through a cocurriculum offering "a substantial faculty presence." The aim is precisely that of "connecting the curricular and cocurricular lives of Willamette students" (Willamette University Office of Campus Life).

Advances in creating connection are not only for residential campuses. Many other examples are appropriate for all types of campuses and student bodies; cultural arts series, international programs, student government, leadership academies, opportunities for volunteer work, art shows, and theater performances are all part of campus life.

Some activities aim for enrichment, while others directly reinforce classroom learning. For example, both faculty members and student affairs staff make efforts to support student media, debate tournaments, Model United Nations, undergraduate research conferences, and other types of projects that require the application of classroom learning in new venues. A number of campuses, such as the University of Texas at El Paso, go one step further by providing students with a supplementary transcript that records their cocurricular accomplishments.

WILLAMETTE UNIVERSITY

SALEM, OREGON

Making Cocurricular Life Connect

Administrators and trustees at Willamette University recognized the educational value of the cocurriculum in a task force report that stated, "we are not well-served if the various college constituencies think in terms of 'academics' vs. social life." In planning campus renovations, the university designed its Kaneko residential commons to include various housing communities that are governed by their residents, a significant faculty presence, and a student center offering films, a lecture series, and experiential learning activities to promote student involvement both in the commons and in the larger Salem community.

Assessment activities also have begun to focus on the cocurriculum, and the results reveal that general education goals such as global understanding, aesthetic appreciation, and oral communication are developed and reinforced in cocurricular activities. In short, strong general education programs acknowledge and work with the cocurriculum.

Visionary Leadership

Strong general education programs begin and end with the faculty. But they do not come into being without astute leadership at all levels—administrators, faculty members, students. A recent Association of American Colleges and Universities publication, *Revising General Education—and Avoiding the Potholes* (Gaston and Gaff 2009), makes clear the importance of administrative leaders who offer conspicuous, well-informed support and of faculty leaders who work astutely within the institution's political environment. The engagement of student leaders in curricular reform can provide a valuable additional dimension. Consistent leadership is necessary to promote revisions as well as to maintain the centrality and vitality of general education.

Effective general education therefore embodies two related principles. First, any curricular reform effort likely to succeed must enjoy the visible backing of the university's administrative leadership. This can take many forms. Adequate funding for the general education offering is, of course, paramount, but a willingness to reassign faculty time to curricular priorities, to support faculty travel to institutions with model programs, and to invest in faculty development sends a strong message. Second, faculty and student leaders must take the politics of such reform seriously by planning approaches likely to secure approval from their colleagues, by anticipating and bridging or circumventing likely potholes, and by dedicating themselves to the necessary follow through. While strong academic programs should be the *sine qua non* for attracting and maintaining support throughout the academic community, those working within and committed to such programs cannot take such support for granted. Strategies to cultivate such support through effective communication and the engagement of important constituencies must represent a continuing priority for those genuinely interested in building and sustaining effective general education programs.

There is no question that it takes time to develop interest and garner support for change. That a politic and savvy approach can be accomplished with reasonable dispatch, however, appears in the process of general education reform pursued by the University of Georgia. A task force on general education and student learning convened in September 2004 reported its recommendations eleven months later, at which point the university mobilized to implement them. In the following year, as a subcommittee met regularly to develop a new general education framework, it regularly shared drafts of its work, sought input from the faculty, and sponsored forums open to all members of the academic community. In the fall of 2006, just two years after the task force first convened, the plan was approved by the university's curricular body, its governance body, and its president. Courses since approved for offering in the new core curriculum are now being taught.

PART THREE: Effective Practices in General Education

Chapter 3
Intentionality
ANN S. FERREN

General education programs should suggest intentionality at every level: the program itself, its constituent elements (first-year programs, learning communities, capstone courses), and individual courses.

In the simplest possible terms, effective general education depends on institutions, faculty members, and students who have a clear idea regarding what is to be accomplished and a deliberate and realistic approach to assuring that accomplishment in fact occurs.

The major impetus for reform of general education some twenty-five years ago was the claim that most programs lacked "coherence" and shared no widely agreed-upon content and skills (AAC 1985). Much of the attention following that critique focused on prescribing "what students should know," and significant debates about specific courses and readings sometimes overshadowed other issues. Institutions with carefully structured programs taught by full-time faculty and focused on first-year seminars, sequenced cores, and integrative themes—such as Columbia University and Saint Joseph's College in Indiana—demonstrated that general education could be a coherent and memorable part of a student's education.

But some programs regarded as exemplary could offer only limited evidence that the educational experiences they offered were indeed superior. *Strong Foundations* (AAC 1994) was the first multicampus study that teased out the elements of effective and sustainable programs and provided examples from many different sizes and types of campuses. The study did not claim that a particular structural element or specific content was better than another, but rather confirmed the importance of faculty engaging in continuous reflective dialogue about the purposes of the program; working together to stress connections across courses, skills, and disciplines; and developing broad community support and leadership to sustain the vitality of a program.

Reform efforts continue to be supported by evidence that students benefit from intentional structures, sequenced learning, good advising, engaging pedagogy, and regular assessment. Studies of the student experience begun in the early 1990s by scholars such as Richard Light and George Kuh have confirmed that all types of students need

ANN S. FERREN *is provost at the American University in Bulgaria. She is the coauthor of* Leadership through Collaboration (*Praeger, 2004*).

guidance in their educational planning so that they experience a clear beginning, middle, and culmination. Thus the term "intentionality" has come to be associated with general education programs that deliberately assist students in their transition from secondary school to college and then guide them through increasingly challenging course work that is connected to the major course of study, to cocurricular experiences, and to personal aspirations (AAC&U 2002).

The most recent work on curricular impact has further clarified that linear development and structure are not enough. Nor can one course or experience bring the desired results (AAC&U 2005). Connections across disciplines are necessary to encourage analytic and integrative thinking. Collaborative work on real-world challenges leads to creativity and problem solving. And multiple opportunities for application and practice reinforce college-level learning and the capacities necessary for lifelong learning. As campuses align outcomes with structural and pedagogical elements, it should not be surprising that many advising documents are no longer checklists of requirements but flow charts and diagrams showing relationships among course clusters, skills, and in-class and out-of-class experiences. The student? At the center!

Students now far more often receive encouragement to build portfolios of their learning experiences according to a guiding schematic that represents their baccalaureate aims. And curricular maps outlining which courses introduce a skill or knowledge area, which courses develop it further, and at what point mastery is expected can enable both faculty members and students to understand how parts are related to the whole. Ideally, advising, assessment, and student services are also designed to help students understand their options in college, the connections among their experiences, and their progress toward learning outcomes. In short, intentionality represents a focused effort to help students be more mindful not only of general education but of all aspects of the college experience.

Intentionality Must Focus on Students

Changes in our understanding of general education have not come easily. Because few faculty members receive preparation in curricular design, pedagogy, or learning theory as part of their graduate education, they tend to rely on their own experience within their own disciplines in organizing and presenting their courses. As Lattuca and Stark observe (2009), it is no wonder, then, that general education reform takes so long. It is difficult to create consensus when faculty members come to the table with different perspectives. For example, the mathematician thinks of curricula as sequential, whereas the teacher of poetry may find prerequisites unimportant. A general education planning group that includes representatives from many disciplines and colleges may find that reaching agreement on a common sense of coherence is a challenge. The only principle shared by the members may be the desire to "protect turf" or ensure that certain courses are included in the proposed program.

In contrast, when faculty members intentionally design curricula around the needs of students in the context of developmental and constructivist learning theories, they may understand that a general education program guided by desired outcomes—such as those defined through the multiyear work of the Association of American Colleges and University's Liberal Education and America's Promise project—is preferable to a program with broad distribution requirements. Institutions that adopt outcomes-directed programs accept their rightful responsibility for coherence and integration rather than simply assume that students will somehow draw together the disparate elements of their educational experience.

Such acceptance of responsibility at the institutional level is especially important given the broad diversity of students and their needs. Although there is little agreement as to the characteristics of the so-called "millennial generation," faculty members cannot ignore the growing impact that social networking, cell phone chatter, and Twittering has on relationships and concepts of time and space. This generation of students has been described as multi-taskers, as pressured to achieve, as confident that they are special, as assertive of their rights, and as fearful of not belonging (Strauss and Howe 2003). In addition, as chapter 1 observed, students are increasingly diverse in age, background, culture, experience, and preparation. In such a complex environment, while there may be no "best" structure for the elements of general education, "any" structure will not do. Strong programs—as they reflect awareness of students' identities, how they access the program, and how they learn—embody institutional intent in connecting options and experiences in meaningful ways for a specific campus and specific learners.

The Importance of the First Year

The wide variety of first-year-experience programs demonstrates how different formats can serve different purposes. Some campuses offer a critical-inquiry seminar on a challenging topic such as climate change to emphasize for students the transition from high school–level to college-level learning. Other campuses help students form a bond with the institution by using small first-year seminars to link advising and coursework. Others stress academic and social development by encouraging students to register for a cluster of courses within a freshman interest group, a small community within the larger university. Increasingly, programs initiated to ease transition and encourage persistence have evolved to include the larger purpose of helping students define their goals from the outset and assume responsibility for pursuing them. Such programs no longer ask, what do we want them to know and be able to do? They ask instead, what do *they* want to know and be able to do? The goal is to help students become intentional about their learning.

The first year also offers important opportunities for students to connect to the larger community beyond the classroom and the institution. Through both individual challenges and collaborative activities, students come to understand themselves more fully, to recognize what can be learned from others, to experience reciprocity and teamwork, and to test their ability to overcome parochial thinking and respect the ideas of others. To help achieve these important outcomes, elements such as service learning, volunteer work, a controversial speaker series, or intentionally diverse learning and living arrangements may be planned for the first year. While not always identified as directly linked to general education, such strategies can support the accomplishment of general education goals.

Within strong general education programs, effective first-year programs serve as a threshold to sustained programming. Unlike campuses disappointed by National Survey of Student Engagement findings suggesting a decline in student engagement after the first year, institutions such as Evergreen State College, Alverno College, and Wagner College sustain a high level of involvement by articulating how expectations established in the first year will be continued throughout the subsequent years of the college career. Assessment activities are used to track effectiveness at the end of each year relative to benchmarks established for each program objective. Monitoring learning sequences through transcript analysis can also reveal whether students are experiencing the gains from the curriculum and cocurriculum that the institution seeks to ensure.

Developing, Extending, and Mastering Transferable Skills

A truism for general education programs is that "the whole should be greater than the sum of the parts." Yet critics of the undergraduate experience find in programs evidence of a good start and a strong finish but a "muddle in the middle." Intentionally designed programs address this concern by framing what should happen not just in the first year but also in the second, third, and fourth years. Education is, as it should be, cumulative, with opportunities for reinforcement at many stages. Of course, for that to happen, faculty members need to work together so that their students can integrate the work they do and build on it from course to course and year to year. For example, Franklin Pierce College organizes its general education requirements sequentially so that all students take them in the same order in the first three years.

Although we know that students learn most effectively from practice, repetition, and multiple exposures, this ideal can be difficult to achieve. It takes time and commitment for faculty members to design courses together, to align their readings and writing assignments, and to incorporate opportunities for application, reflection, and reinforcement. It has always been easier just to add—rather than integrate—new elements to the curriculum. For example, instead of integrating race, class, gender, and cross-cultural concerns systemically within the curriculum, many campuses have simply added diversity and international courses. And rather than expect every faculty member to teach written and oral communication skills, as a comprehensive approach would require, some campuses add writing-intensive courses to the disciplines. By avoiding the obligation to work intentionally with regard to the curriculum as a whole, reform committees may avoid the resistance that more significant change could arouse. But they—and their students—will miss the advantages that follow from a more holistic approach.

The challenge of providing multiple opportunities to develop and reinforce learning is even greater for campuses that receive transfer students who will miss some of the important elements at the desired stage, such as the first-year seminar. Other structures such as clustered courses, sequenced courses, and linked courses can ensure that even late arrivals will benefit from thoughtful, well-integrated curricular choices. American

University offers a two-course sequence in each of its five Modes of Inquiry to allow greater study in depth, an approach modeled after prerequisites that provide thresholds to majors. Similarly, City University of New York–Brooklyn College organizes its program into two tiers, so that transfer students enter at the appropriate level based on their previous credits earned—perhaps foregoing a lower-tier course like Shaping of the Modern World, but taking a Global Connections course in the upper tier, such as The Development of the Silk Road. Through such approaches, transfer students can more readily make connections between what they have studied elsewhere and the intentional elements of their new academic program.

Coherence In and Among Individual Courses

Students who ask, why isn't a general education course just general instead of being so difficult? fail to understand the relationship of general education to their other coursework. A recent AAC&U survey of institutions found that only 42 percent of respondents indicated that "almost all or a majority" of students understood the role of their institution's stated learning outcomes (Hart Research Associates 2009). Attempting to answer the question by renaming the program as "Liberal Learning" or "The Core," as some institutions have done, may send the right message but still fall short of intentionality. Strong programs pay attention to good public relations with students, to be sure, but they emphasize above all student understanding of the scaffold of learning built through a sequence of related courses and cumulative experiences.

Of course, for understanding to become possible, the scaffolding must exist. And in too many colleges and universities, the curriculum reflects not a deliberate structure but an amalgam created through accretion. The course catalog then serves, in Lee Knefelkamp's well-known phrase, as a campus "autobiography," the legacy created by faculty members who have come and gone over the years. Even if there are policies governing the removal from the catalog of seldom offered courses or a requirement that syllabi must be kept current, a lack of intentionality may appear when accrediting agencies or internal program review processes require the systematic mapping of educational outcomes. In such instances, external evaluators may be able to detect idiosyncrasies difficult for those on a campus to see. Faculty who strive for intentionality would do well to review all of the prevailing paradigms: assumptions about prerequisites, what course level designations and course numberings signify, and the extent to which course workloads and outcomes are aligned with the award of credits.

George Kuh's work on levels of challenge using results from the National Survey of Student Engagement revealed varying expectations across a wide sample of campuses about the work faculty expected of students. Clearly, on each campus, students would benefit from faculty members working together to establish shared criteria: What is the writing expectation in a 200-level course? How much reading should students do in a course at the first level? What makes a special topics course "advanced"? To address such questions requires not only an understanding of what questions to ask, but also a framework for dealing with the answers. Typically, a strong faculty development program and

---

CITY UNIVERSITY OF NEW YORK BROOKLYN COLLEGE

BROOKLYN, NEW YORK

Integrating Transfer Students' Experience

At Brooklyn College, the general education program is arranged in two tiers, so that transfer students enter at the appropriate level based on their previous credits earned. This arrangement allows transfer students to more readily make connections between what they have learned at previous institutions and the intentional elements of their new program.

well-designed program review processes are necessary conditions to support intentionality within a general education program, as well as across the curriculum.

A more ambitious effort modeled after the Bologna Process, which aims to ensure comparable learning outcomes across the European Higher Education Area, has been taking place under the auspices of the Lumina Foundation in three states: Minnesota, Indiana, and Utah. There, faculty members in selected disciplines have convened statewide to attempt to reach consensus on learning and capability levels applicable to their respective disciplines. The frameworks that result from this process are used to achieve comparability and transparency across institutions or states. While this "tuning" process focuses primarily on outcomes of the major, skills such as critical thinking and oral and written communication drawn from general education also are essential to employability and lifelong learning. Perhaps in the future, some combination of national, statewide, and campus efforts will enable the academy to be clear about what it seeks to accomplish and intentional about how it "intends" to do so.

As campuses more intentionally link general education to the major, they strengthen awareness of a vertical spine running through the four years of college. For example, the University of Hartford uses a sequenced building-block model in its engineering program to align general education courses with each stage of the major. Faculty collaborate across the involved disciplines at each step so that students take the general education courses in a predictable order, not at random, and can build upon perspectives and skills from previous years. Any campus can balance the demands of a cumulative general education program with those of electives and the major by looking for appropriate connections. Those that create such alignments throughout the four-year baccalaureate curriculum no longer encourage their students to "get general education out of the way" so that serious application to the major may commence.

Integrating Experiences and Outcomes in the Final Year

Some years back, the higher education community began to ask, what is special about the senior year? How can we help students draw together their experiences, integrate their learning, and prepare for the transition to graduate school or employment? Many campuses already had capstone experiences within majors, such as a senior thesis or a senior seminar, but such courses or activities had a limited purpose—for example, determining which students would graduate with honors. Attention to the capstone has now become an important element in intentional curricular design and may lead to broader and more inclusive expectations. The structure of such experiences may differ—and may include an internship, senior project, thesis, or seminar offered either to individuals or groups—but within intentional curricula, the goals now tend to be far broader. Through the active learning involved in a project or seminar, students work with faculty as supervisors or mentors to gain an integrated perspective on their baccalaureate experience as a whole.

Through the active learning involved in a project or seminar, students work with faculty as supervisors or mentors to gain an integrated perspective on their baccalaureate

---

WORCESTER POLYTECHNIC INSTITUTE

WORCESTER, MASSACHUSETTS

Tackling Complex Real-World Problems

Students at Worcester Polytechnic Institute complete an Interactive Qualifying Project in the junior or senior year, taking on a tough technological problem with human and social dimensions. The students work in interdisciplinary teams, often with an external organization, to develop solutions to problems facing diverse communities. Students can complete the project in the United States or at one of fourteen international centers, and may work on the task full time for one semester, or across three terms as part of the standard course load.

experience as a whole. One of the most ambitious undertakings is at Worcester Polytechnic Institute, where the senior Interactive Qualifying Project is linked with study abroad. The project poses a complex technological problem with human and social dimensions that requires the integration of skills and knowledge developed in both general education and the major. Students interested in strengthening their global perspective can choose to undertake the project at one of fourteen international project centers.

Although the majority of such senior-year experiences remain in the domain of the major, a number of campuses have developed a discrete capstone or senior-year experience that is identified as part of the overall liberal learning plan. Wagner College requires a third learning community experience with a reflective tutorial and project at the senior level to integrate outcomes from the major with liberal learning outcomes. Saint Joseph's College in Indiana continues its thematic seminar program into the senior year to strengthen the college's overall goals. Some campuses, such as the University of Connecticut, focus on the transition from college to the workplace and include an array of curricular and cocurricular experiences. Whatever the approach taken, broader attention to culmination and transition can contribute significantly to the coherence of the curriculum and the preparation of students for employment or graduate study.

Yet of all elements of an intentionally designed general education program, the senior-year experience as an intentional element of general education—as opposed to the major—appears to be the least widely implemented. One reason may lie in the extent to which a capstone experience calls for a different type of involvement and commitment on the part of students and faculty members. Indeed, many report that a totally different relationship develops as they work together in a mentoring relationship on a research project or integrative seminar. Research confirms that this mentoring relationship has a deep impact on not only the students' learning but also their understanding of themselves as learners. Students who undertake a demanding project often report afterward that they had not been aware of their capacity for collaborative investigation of a high quality. And a faculty member whose collegial relationship with a student results in substantive project outcomes or a conference presentation contributes significantly to the students' transition to graduate study or employment.

Integrating In-Class and Out-of-Class Experiences

As campuses recognize that outcomes attributed to the baccalaureate degree are not accomplished only within academic settings, intentional collaboration among academic affairs, student affairs, and other constituencies leads to cooperative projects that serve student learning. Choosing a broadly assigned book or theme for the academic year, holding a campuswide lecture series, scheduling class meetings in residence halls, mounting cocurricular community-based projects that extend throughout the year—such undertakings can involve faculty members, staff members, and students in integrated in-class and out-of-class experiences. Because most students spend less than 15 percent of their waking hours in a classroom, there are many hours available for cocurricular activities, recreation, work, and other responsibilities. Strong programs are intentional about offering linkages to strengthen the overall learning experience.

> **TULANE UNIVERSITY**
> NEW ORLEANS, LOUISIANA
>
> **Service as a Way of Life**
>
> Tulane University renewed its focus on community involvement following Hurricane Katrina, which devastated the university's local community. Students are now mandated to complete a public service project, which is administered through the university's Center for Public Service. The requirement spans the entire educational experience, with students taking service-learning courses within the first two years, and completing a final service-learning project, internship, or service-based study abroad experience during the junior or senior year.

To be sure, residential campuses have an advantage in connecting cocurricular experiences to classroom learning. The research evidence is clear. The more engaged and active a student is in the community, the more powerful the total educational experience. Even demanding commitments to work or to intercollegiate athletics appear to enhance—rather than detract from—liberal and professional learning (Light 2001). As noted in chapter 1, workers who study, as distinct from students who work, represent a majority on an increasing number of campuses. Thus, the challenge for campuses is to make work experience a part of the guided educational plan.

Making such connections is far more challenging for commuter campuses and for institutions that enroll many nontraditional-aged students with many off-campus responsibilities. Many community colleges are taking advantage of portfolios, learning communities, and other structures to help students and faculty make stronger connections.

One approach that appears to work for many different types of institutions is that of guided community engagement, the linking of academic work in the classroom to powerful out-of-class experiences. Tulane University, which renewed its focus on community involvement following Hurricane Katrina, mandates that all students complete a public service requirement, administered by the university's Center for Public Service. Separated into two sequential parts, the requirement ensures that students have a "cumulative and reflective" experience. Within their first two years, students enroll in a service-learning class, and during the junior or senior year, they complete a final project, which could include an academic service-learning internship, a public service honors thesis project, or a service-based international study abroad program (Tulane University).

In all such cases, students who complete their work in an off-campus setting develop a relationship with their supervisor and colleagues that is quite different from most on-campus relationships. Indeed, one common theme from faculty members and supervisors who take part in such projects is deep respect for what a student can do. Students comment similarly on the exhilaration arising from applying what they have learned in the classroom to issues in the real world.

The Common Thread

From the design of the general education program itself, to the alignment of general education and the major, to first-year and senior-year opportunities for integration and application, the single most conspicuous determinant of quality can be summarized in a single word: intentionality. Strong baccalaureate programs do not emerge through accretion year by year. Liberal learning outcomes are not met through programs that simply evolve. The high calling of offering education and enabling learning requires nothing less than the deliberate, focused attention of all those involved. To reach consensus on intent and on the strategies that will enable the accomplishment of that intent—that is the challenge colleagues share. And it is their professional responsibility to share it with each other and their students.

Chapter 4
Alignment with the Majors
KAREN MAITLAND SCHILLING AND DWIGHT SMITH

General education programs, well aligned with majors, should express a comprehensive institutional commitment to the liberal education of all students by means of the entire curriculum.

In the concluding paragraphs of *Strong Foundations*, the authors asserted that general education had at last "come of age." Aligning themselves with higher education leaders, they described general education as "both a rich concept and a continuing ideal" (AAC 1994, 57). The evidence in support of this assertion continues to accumulate. The survey of Association of American Colleges and Universities member institutions conducted by Hart Research Associates (2009) reported that a majority of institutions (1) have a common set of intended learning outcomes for their undergraduate students; (2) have identified general education as an institutional priority; and (3) are in some stage of assessing or modifying their general education program. Moreover, student learning outcomes identified as important in an employer survey conducted for AAC&U in 2006 mirror closely the outcomes that institutions say they intend for their graduates (Peter D. Hart Research Associates 2007). These overarching competencies, such as critical thinking or teamwork, are now recognized by employers as of an importance commensurate to those accomplished within the major.

That is the good news. Where concerns arise is from our awareness that these outcomes are not always accomplished. Indeed, the increasing effectiveness of assessment on college campuses, as detailed in chapter 6, has demonstrated the importance of integration within general education, between a general education and major programs, and between the curriculum and the cocurriculum. Programs that invite students to choose among a bewildering variety of options without requiring educational designs that are coherent, integrative, and pragmatic are likely to face a challenge in demonstrating measurable educational gains. To the contrary, as assessment has helped us understand more about student learning, it has also shown us that if our students are to achieve the liberal learning we promise, the members of academy must collaborate to ensure the effectiveness of both the curriculum and the cocurriculum.

KAREN MAITLAND SCHILLING *is dean of the College of Arts and Science and professor of psychology at Miami University.*

DWIGHT SMITH *is vice president of academic affairs at the County College of Morris in New Jersey.*

Emerging Conceptions of the Scope of Liberal Learning

The authors of *Strong Foundations* commented favorably on an emerging erosion in the historical distinction between breadth, associated traditionally with general education, and depth, associated with study in the major. And we continue to observe in strong programs the preference for synergy over duality, the concerted pursuit of breadth *with* depth, and the recognition that study within general education can include advanced discovery and that study in the major can be foundational.

Increasingly, faculty members are recognizing the importance of "scaffolding" in the design of curricula. Teachers of writing have long argued that the complex skills and competencies required by a new century develop only through incremental emphasis, but we have come to realize that all essential learning develops most fully through work that is cumulative, integrative, and reflective. Similarly, quantitative literacy, once relegated to foundation courses, should be developed incrementally throughout many courses. And research, once expected only of mature students in advanced courses, now appears in many first-year programs. Dated notions of specific outcomes attached to "my course" for "my students" have in strong programs given way to emphases on partnering to achieve a cumulative impact.

Witness the growing emphasis on liberal learning goals in such professional education programs as business, engineering, and nursing. Indeed, programmatic accreditors in these professions have defined desired outcomes that are often closely aligned with institutional general education goals. Precisely because of this linkage of liberal learning outcomes and professional outcomes, the increasing career orientation of students no longer weighs against their achieving the goals of liberal learning. As a result, faculty teaching in professional programs who once saw general education as unrelated now are likely to see both the courses and competencies as integral to their goals. Many document this integration in their accreditation self-studies.

Challenges and Supports for Comprehensive Programs

Even the most salutary institutional commitment must operate in the real world. As observed in chapter 1, the educational landscape has changed and continues to change, and many assumptions serviceable enough in the twentieth century no longer hold. Most institutions today must deal with a "swirl" of students. As Adelman's (1999) analysis of students' college transcripts suggests, even a "traditional" student living in an on-campus residence hall may attend class on campus in the morning, address the requirements of an asynchronous course offered by an online provider in the afternoon, and drive across town that evening to take a community college course that will satisfy the home institution's degree requirements. Because more and more students now complete their general education requirements at a community college or some other institution before transferring to the institution from which they will seek the baccalaureate, baccalaureate institutions must focus on ensuring that all of their graduates enjoy the benefit of a coordinated and intentional approach to well-integrated learning goals.

Faculty teaching in professional programs who once saw general education as unrelated now are likely to see both the courses and competencies as integral to their goals.

Since 2000, Arkansas, California, Connecticut, Iowa, Louisiana, Maine, Missouri, Nevada, New Jersey, New Mexico, Oregon, Tennessee, Texas, Virginia, Utah, and Washington have enacted laws to facilitate the seamless transfer of credit between public institutions of higher education (B. Vandel, pers. comm.). Florida and Illinois have previously established general education articulation requirements between their public higher education institutions, and in Florida even private institutions have the opportunity to participate voluntarily in the state's course articulation system.

In states such as Florida, Utah, and New Jersey, where general education course requirements are prescribed according to curricular categories and the number of credits for each, the conversation about alignment between general education and the major has moved beyond a single institution to all institutions within the state. The broadly shared responsibility for general education and the state-mandated discussions among faculty within disciplines would in all likelihood advance the cause of coherence and intentionality in the pursuit of liberal learning for all students if only the statewide approaches were not based on very dated notions of general education. In general, these approaches convene faculty to focus on providing breadth of content at the foundational level. The alignment of general education with institutional mission, the framing of structures that relate general education to the major more closely, the encouragement of innovation in the juxtaposition of the curriculum and cocurriculum—such opportunities to make significant advances in the effectiveness of general education so as to ensure the advantages of liberal learning for all students may not find fertile soil in legislated uniformity.

Statewide agreements based on conventional assumptions of the twentieth century may weigh against reform, but when such agreements are well informed by innovative thinking and good practice they can exert a powerful stimulus within higher education. There are other helpful initiatives to guide institutions. The Association of American Colleges and Universities, through its Liberal Education and America's Promise initiative, offers progressive counsel to system articulation efforts by moving the conversation beyond agreement on the equivalence of inputs to consensus on shared outcomes for student learning. Current efforts by the Teagle Foundation to foster consensus on learning outcomes for students in specific majors also provide more contemporary models for alignment and articulation between general education and the major.

Faculty Roles and Responsibilities

Another traditional assumption with regard to curriculum review and revision processes has been that the responsibility rests principally with full-time faculty. But as observed in chapter 1, here too current reality may intrude. Recent analyses indicate that, in 2007, the number of full-time tenured or tenure-track faculty accounted for just over 30 percent of all faculty on campuses throughout the country (American Association of University Professors 2009). As a consequence, at many institutions general education courses are increasingly the purview of non-tenure-track faculty, adjuncts, "road scholars" (who may teach three or four courses at three or four different institutions), and graduate assistants. Some higher education institutions have even outsourced the teaching of general education courses to online providers. In such instances, general education reform initiatives that engage only full-time tenured and tenure-track faculty may fail to incorporate the important insights of those most directly involved in the program.

A related issue appears in institutional standards for awarding tenure or promotion to full-time faculty and continuing the contracts of adjunct and non-tenure-track instructors. From one college or university to another, we can observe considerable variation in the value accorded to the teaching of general education courses and to participation in the reform and maintenance of general education programs. An institutional commitment to explicit general education outcomes would suggest that high-quality faculty participation in general education would receive favorable attention in the promotion and tenure process, but this is not always the case. In fact, one large state university in Ohio, which had earlier adopted a broader definition of scholarship to signal a higher value placed on participation in curricular design and implementation, recently reverted to the traditional "teaching/research/service" rubric so as to restore an overriding emphasis on research. Because institutional priorities are often stated most influentially in the language of evaluative rubrics and career rewards, it is important that institutions determined to ensure liberal learning outcomes for all students attempt some degree of consistency between the ends they seek and the incentives they offer to those most responsible for achieving those ends.

Student Preparedness and Expectations

The wide variation found in student preparedness for college has been well documented. At one regional campus in New Mexico, fully 95 percent of matriculating students are assigned to one or more transitional courses that must be completed prior to college-level study. However, as important as competence in writing, mathematics, and other subject areas is, students prepared to do well in college also require a clear understanding of the expectations that will greet them, of the liberal learning outcomes they will be asked to accomplish, and of the relationship of both general education and the major to such outcomes. Stanford University's Bridge Project found that first-generation students, especially, are likely to enter college without such awareness (Venezia, Kirst, and Antonio 2004). To many of them, learning outcomes for general education and the major may be alien concepts. And the experience that they have once in college may tend to reinforce, rather than temper, their insecurity and uncertainty.

For instance, nearly all institutions of higher learning identify competence in written communication as one of the important liberal learning outcomes. But most students first encounter this expectation through one or two courses in composition taught through the auspices of the English department. And while many institutions appear to assume that such foundational courses will prepare students for the writing they will be asked to do in other courses and in the major, the student experience may be quite different. Differences in priority, in style, and in conventional forms are widespread among the disciplines. Intentional programs provide guidance and seek to align general education with the major. They embody attention to the kinds of writing assignments offered to beginning students as well as to those at advanced stages of their programs. And they make clear the standards by which such assignments are evaluated and the ways in which evaluations are communicated.

Tools like curriculum maps and scoring rubrics, such as those described by Maki (2004), may be helpful to the communication of learning outcomes throughout the general education and major programs. Institutions such as Miami Dade College have used curriculum mapping to document where within the curriculum learning outcomes are introduced and reinforced in both the general education program and the majors. In short, expectations must be made explicit to students throughout the curriculum, whether in general education or major courses.

Alignment in the Context of Accreditation and Accountability Demands

The extent to which the essential learning outcomes of liberal education are accomplished throughout the general education and major programs can be illuminated by assessment. The challenge for conducting such assessment is to obtain and interpret information that will in fact shed light on how well the outcomes are accomplished overall and not just in parts of the curriculum. The information obtained guides the alignment of general education and the major and a commitment to continuous improvement.

Alignment also stands at the center of assessment and accountability requirements as defined for both general education and major programs, a convergence seen in shared expectations among regional and specialized program accreditors. Because the assessment of learning outcomes, such as written communication, is encouraged or required by both types of accreditors, faculty members must take this expectation seriously whether they are engaged principally in general education courses or in those specific to a major. Similarly, because some accreditors, such as ABET (engineering and technology) and the Association to Advance Collegiate Schools of Business (business), expect to find some evidence of study in depth within the general education curriculum, faculty members have another strong incentive to collaborate on general education reforms that serve well the alignment of general education with the disciplines.

Both regional and specialized accreditors now routinely audit programs and institutions for their commitment to both effective assessment and the use of assessment as part of an "accountability loop" supporting a commitment to continuous improvement. Their shared interest in this indicator of institutional quality represents a strong incentive for those concerned with the closer alignment of general education and the major.

Alignment as Institutional Commitment

The alignment of general education and the major is an important means to an important end—but it is, finally, a means. The end lies in an institutional commitment to liberal learning for all students through an intentional, well-coordinated curriculum. Hence, discussion of alignment must in due course turn to those institutional commitments required for the means to those necessary to secure the end.

1. **An institutional commitment to understanding students.** Following students as they navigate their way through the curriculum provides the opportunity for faculty and administrators to understand student expectations more fully and to gauge student preparedness more accurately. For some institutions, the results may be surprising. Venerable assumptions about the student body may, in fact, have to give way to a more accurate understanding of students who spend less time on campus and more time on the job, and of students who are more likely to transfer—both into and out of the institution. These factors necessarily make the alignment of general education and the major a more complex undertaking.
2. **An institutional commitment to systems of higher education.** Because of demographic, economic, and social changes reflected in the student body, and in some cases because of changes in state law, the alignment of general education and the major must serve students who transfer in and out of the institution. Hence, the challenge is one that institutions cannot address in isolation. Sound articulation arrangements among institutions and within states, which must necessarily help define the relationship between general education and the major, thus depend on mutual respect among different types of institutions and their faculty and administrators.
3. **An institutional commitment to the value of tenured and tenure-track faculty teaching general education courses.** In the faculty hiring, promotion, and tenure processes, an institution should make explicit the value it places on the teaching of general education. An institution committed to teaching also welcomes faculty engagement in the scholarship of teaching and learning. How effectively a faculty member teaches general education courses should represent an important factor in faculty reviews, whether the faculty member is tenured, tenure track, or adjunct. And a temptation to outsource the teaching of general education courses should be weighed against the institution's commitment to the alignment of general education and the major.
4. **An institutional commitment to use assessment results to understand student achievement of essential outcomes, for the benefit of faculty, administrators, and students.** Assessment, discussed later in this volume in more detail, can serve the alignment of general education and the major in several ways—for example, by measuring the effectiveness of alternate structures, by gauging the quality of preparation for specific majors provided by general education, and by comparing student success in general education with that in the major. Assessment results can also enable students to identify their learning strengths and their opportunities for improvement, both with respect to the essential outcomes of liberal learning and with respect to outcomes specific to particular majors. Moreover, when an institution embraces assessment and accountability reporting requirements in order to communicate more effectively with prospective students about its expectations, students may arrive more fully prepared to succeed.

Offering the benefits of liberal education in this new century to all students will challenge all types of higher education institutions. These commitments can serve as a guide toward the institutional focus necessary to improve student learning in general education and in major programs.

Chapter 5

Effective Pedagogy
J. ELIZABETH CLARK

General education programs should incorporate effective pedagogies throughout their curricula, with particular focus on crossing disciplinary boundaries, putting students at the center of learning, and including reflective meaning-making exercises to ensure students understand their progress.

Faculty members today often find themselves on the divide between twenty-first-century expectations and twentieth-century conventions and facilities. There may be no better illustration of this challenge than Michael Wesch's Digital Ethnography project at Kansas State University. Participating students document the realities of their lives with video cameras, filming the way they access information and learn, their loci for social and professional interactions, and their increasing dependence on digital technology, while sitting in the anonymous molded plastic seats of a traditional lecture hall (Wesch 2007). As students examine digital technology, they encounter both the limitations of their present educational environments and the effective pedagogies that can now guide student learning. Harnessing current technologies to engage student scholars as co-inquirers, Wesch's pedagogical approach confronts squarely the demands of today's changing global community. But he is in some ways an exception. Too often, higher education remains unprepared to teach those who have grown up with technology and have been educated in high schools like the city of Philadelphia's School of the Future, which offers a project-based curriculum supported by virtual and face-to-face interactions between faculty members and students.

Crossing Boundaries

Increasingly, faculty members are being asked to work collaboratively across disciplines to create environments that embody the interdisciplinarity of knowledge. Clearly, global problems such as pandemics, natural disasters, and political crises may be addressed only through the synergy of multiple disciplines. As faculty members pursue integrative learning across the curriculum, they move beyond the paradigm of "course outcomes" to an understanding of how individual courses contribute to a larger educational whole.

J. ELIZABETH CLARK *is professor of English at LaGuardia Community College/City University of New York. Her most recent article in* Computers and Composition, *"The Digital Imperative," examines the use of educational technology, such as e-portfolios and blogs, in the writing classroom.*

It should not therefore be surprising, as Mary Huber and Pat Hutchings demonstrate in *Integrative Learning: Mapping the Terrain* (2004), that enabling undergraduates to overcome curricular fragmentation and connect their learning "is becoming a priority at many colleges and universities."

Otterbein College prepares students for an interconnected global community through an integrative studies program intended to help them use their learning to "serve and shape [their] chosen responsibilities in and to the world." By connecting individual learning with global and cultural knowledge, Otterbein teaches key skills such as ethics, public engagement, social responsibility, critical thinking, and intercultural knowledge as it prompts "intellectual curiosity about the world as it is and a deeper understanding of the global condition" (Otterbein College).

Portland State University's capstone course offers another model for integrative learning by placing students on interdisciplinary teams to apply what they have learned "to a real challenge emanating from the metropolitan community" (Portland State University). Recent group projects have ranged from the creation of public service Web sites about colon cancer and melanoma to environmental projects examining the effects of motor vehicles on the atmosphere.

Both Otterbein's and Portland State's programs rely on a pedagogy that works outside of traditional disciplinary boundaries and encourages students to explore connections between courses, disciplines, and cocurricular experiences. The Association of American Colleges and Universities' Liberal Education and America's Promise project report (2007) and George Kuh's *High-Impact Educational Practices* (2008) offer other examples of ways to align pedagogies with desired outcomes.

Putting Students at the Center of Learning

New pedagogies place students at the center of learning. Reflecting standards articulated in *Strong Foundations* (AAC 1994), effective classrooms invite students as learners—not receivers—by engaging them in the discovery of new knowledge and enabling them to showcase their best work. At colleges as diverse as LaGuardia Community College, Clemson University, San Francisco State University, the University of Michigan, the University of Oregon, and Virginia Polytechnic Institute and State University, students display their work, argue for their findings, and publish portfolios—both paper and electronic—that demonstrate connections among their courses, professional goals, cocurricular activities, and academic achievements.

For her students in courses such as environmental science, human and physical geography, and environmental science, Karen Kirk at Montana State University advocates hands-on experiences because they necessitate learning through multiple disciplines and modalities. Kirk says that "experience-based learning allows students to actually live the experiment." Whether the focus is on local issues such as zoning, land use, and local politics or on global issues such as resource extraction and greenhouse emissions, experience-based projects confront students with different learning modalities appropriate to the material and, again, place them at the center (Kirk).

Faculty members use a variety of methods in many different disciplines to support student engagement. A sometimes bewildering variety of approaches has evolved to include reflection, fieldwork, student research, interactive lectures, project-based learning, virtual worlds, games, simulations, visualization, labs, presentations, role playing, I-reporter projects, simulation-based learning, collaborative learning, inquiry-based projects, Socratic questioning, group work, and independent research, but all have in common a determination to place students at the center of the learning process. Many of these standard pedagogies are now being enhanced with new technologies, updating the mode of delivery but not the intent behind the pedagogy.

Not Just Grades, But Meaning

At St. Lawrence University in a first-year program-course, students write reflective journals and "advising letters" as a way to find additional meaning in their learning. They are by no means singular. At Alverno College, Rose-Hulman Institute of Technology, Kapi'olani Community College, and Spelman College—to name just a few—students develop portfolios that make such learning transparent and that support assessment at the student, programmatic, and college levels. By demonstrating their competencies in designated outcome areas, often reflecting on their own progress as learners, students consider their learning in a structured fashion and in the context of artifacts from their educational experiences. Most significantly, students make meaning from their work, reflecting on their growth and development, noting significant accomplishments. AAC&U's work on its Valid Assessment of Learning in Undergraduate Education project [3] also demonstrates new potential for institutions to collaborate with students, by bringing them into a multifaceted and rich discussion of cross-institutional learning and assessment. Putting students at the center of their own learning includes inviting them into the realm of assessment, encouraging them to document and reflect on their growth as emerging scholars and researchers in the field.

Digital Realities, Digital Pedagogies

By experimenting with new media, many "early adopter" faculty members are collaborating in the development of a digital educational culture. However, their efforts have not yet begun to alter significantly our traditional expectations about classrooms. An increasing misalignment between the curriculum and the culture can disadvantage students who will enter organizations dependent on new technologies. Too often, as Wesch's project demonstrates, today's classrooms may fail to prepare students for a world where the dominance of print-text literacy is increasingly under challenge. Facilitators of strong general education programs understand the need to reflect on traditional paradigms,

Alverno College
Milwaukee, Wisconsin

Integrating Assessment in Learning

Alverno has a strong "ability-based education" system that requires students to demonstrate competency in a particular area through assessments collected in a learning portfolio. The college does not use traditional assessments like exams, and students track their progress through a digital portfolio system that includes feedback from professors, outside experts, and peers. Faculty feedback and students' own reflection on their work creates "a continuous process that improves learning and integrates it with assessment."

---

3 As part of AAC&U's Valid Assessment of Learning in Undergraduate Education project, teams of faculty and other academic and student affairs professionals engaged in an iterative process over eighteen months wherein they gathered, analyzed, synthesized, and then drafted institutional-level rubrics (and related materials) for fifteen of the AAC&U essential learning outcomes. These rubrics are available online at www.aacu.org/value/rubrics.

from curriculum to content to structure to pedagogy, so that they more effectively prepare students for the world they will enter when they graduate.

Supportive technology in all classes—from course management systems to e-portfolios to digital stories to use of multimedia—should represent part of a larger understanding of what it means to learn and produce knowledge in the twenty-first century. Students need to learn both how to use these technological tools to gather information and to author their own multimodal works. Institutions with strong general education programs consider what it means to educate and be educated in an age of information that presents radical challenges to an industrial-era educational model.

Around the country, various interdisciplinary projects have emerged to examine and experiment with emerging technologies. Programs such as the University of Texas at Austin's Computer Writing and Research Lab, Michigan State University's Media Interface and Network Designs Lab and Writing in Digital Environments Research Center, and the University of California-Los Angeles Center for Digital Humanities are forerunners in exploring a digital culture of communication. Moreover, as more high schools adapt their curricula to the possibilities of new technologies, traditional classrooms in higher education may become more and more removed from the pedagogical present.

In short, strong general education programs track the continuing changes in technology, weigh the implications of such changes for pedagogy, adopt tools likely to prove useful in the present, remain receptive to tools likely to prove useful in the future, and, above all, maintain a consistent focus on students.

Providing Support for Pedagogical Change

Despite years of consistent research on the efficacy of pedagogies that engage students, a glance into many classrooms will find faculty members lecturing. New pedagogies win converts slowly. Technology can threaten those who feel themselves to be less than proficient in its use. To create general education programs worthy of today's students requires improved support for faculty so that all may appreciate more fully the opportunities for learning that are emerging through integrative pedagogy and technology. And faculty members engaged in reengineering their approach to the classroom must be encouraged to reflect on their experience and to share that experience with their peers. Professional reflection can create more engaged teaching, more engaged learners, and a more sophisticated understanding of pedagogy in higher education.

Greater attention to what faculty need will lead campuses beyond the issue of "continuing support for faculty" broached in *Strong Foundations* to the question of, what is the right *kind* of support? To be sure, opportunities for professional development, the encouragement of interdisciplinary conversations, and the like are critical, both for their own sake and as an indication of institutional support for faculty growth. But institutions determined to provide liberal learning to all students as effectively and invitingly as possible cannot rely solely on providing "opportunities" for faculty development. Clearer expectations, incentives, and heightened accountability can all play roles in ensuring that faculty become and remain current with regard to new pedagogies and developing tools.

The Professors of the Year selected by the Carnegie Foundation for the Advancement of Teaching often embody emerging principles in undergraduate education. While teaching at very different institutions, these professors share a commitment to engaged pedagogies and scholarly research on teaching and learning. Their work is among the best in the country as they find new ways to situate teaching and learning at the heart of their research and their work with students. They seek to build communities of active practitioners, introducing students to research in the field and soliciting their help in building communal, collaborative work that concretely assists the local community. Another common feature of their engaged pedagogy is the ability to connect theoretical concepts to students' own lives, providing them with a critical lens through which to examine their experiences and choices. These faculty members are comfortable with interdisciplinarity, borrowing a concept from one discipline and using it in another. They effectively choose the best pedagogy for the particular course or lesson, rather than being limited by traditional boundaries and constraints. Above all, these award-winning faculty members consistently demonstrate their keen ability as reflective practitioners, seeking to learn from their own classrooms and experiences with students.

Several institutions are modeling the kinds of faculty support that lead to the kinds of teaching exemplified in the Carnegie Professors of the Year program. For instance, Oklahoma City University has piloted a novel approach to faculty development through its Priddy Fellows staff development program, a collaboration between the university's arts center and its Center for Excellence in Teaching and Learning. Priddy Fellows are selected based on their interest in integrating the arts into their subject-area teaching and participate in a yearlong faculty development program in a learning-community model. Fellows attend a weeklong arts immersion workshop and meet regularly to discuss common readings and to develop arts-integrated curricula for their disciplines. By year's end, each fellow has prepared a new course integrating art with whatever his or her disciplinary area may be. Similarly, at Kent State University, Moulton Scholars from throughout the university's eight-campus system regularly convene with other scholars in their cohort for reflection on pedagogical issues and for work with consultants to develop courses rich in the creative use of technology. Alumni of each program concur that the learning community model promotes reflection about teaching, encourages interdisciplinary collaboration, and supports the assessment of pedagogical effectiveness.

Award-winning faculty members consistently demonstrate their keen ability as reflective practitioners, seeking to learn from their own classrooms and experiences with students.

Chapter 6

Assessment

Peggy Maki

General education programs should document their effectiveness and demonstrate a dynamic commitment to continuous improvement through the articulation of clear learning outcomes and assessment relative to such outcomes.

Coherent and intentional general education programs translate an institution's liberal learning mission into the fabric of institutional life and into the fabric of students' cumulative learning over time. Similarly, shared understanding among educators and shared understanding among students about the educational purposes of their general education curriculum and their relevance to learning in a major program of study are essential. To support these vital characteristics, the periodic assessment of student work must become a rhythm of institutional life—a way of ascertaining how well students are progressing toward and then achieving institutional expectations for student learning. Evidence thus obtained regarding underperforming program elements can prompt collaborative discussion, leading to ways to improve students' achievement. Like every other important practice in effective general education, assessment is focused on students—on making their learning richer and more effective, and on helping them succeed.

Beginning with the Ends

Translating a general education mission into the fabric of institutional life begins when educators work together across an institution to articulate a set of learning outcome statements—sentences that describe what students should be able to demonstrate (1) as a result of their general education program of study, and (2) as a result of integrating general education outcomes into the disciplinary and interdisciplinary contexts of their major programs. Outcome statements explain to students what an institution expects they should be able to achieve based on the coherent design of the general education curriculum and the alignment of that design with major programs and the

Peggy Maki *is an international education consultant specializing in the assessment of student learning, and a former senior scholar at the American Association for Higher Education. Her most recent books are* Assessing for Learning: Building a Sustainable Commitment Across the Institution *(Stylus, 2nd ed., 2010) and* Coming to Terms with Assessing Student Learning *(Stylus, 2010).*

programs and services offered in the cocurriculum. If they do not share an understanding of the aims of a general education program, both educators and students will develop different views of its significance.

As noted in chapter 1, the Association of American Colleges and University's Liberal Education and America's Promise initiative has identified four domains of learning outcomes statements—knowledge of human culture and the physical and natural world; intellectual and practical skills; personal and social responsibility; and integrative and applied learning—that reflect the aims of liberal learning throughout U.S. higher education and that therefore drive the design and assessment of general education. When stitched across students' lives of learning in both the curriculum and cocurriculum, such outcomes become a measure for offering to students multiple opportunities for them to apply and build on their learning.

For example, an institution's focus on quantitative literacy as an outcome of general education should appear again in a student's major program of study as a disciplinary outcome. Students should be asked to apply quantitative reasoning to solve problems in history, the quantitative skills essential to nursing should receive regular reinforcement, and journalism students should receive assignments requiring them to make quantitative analyses. To restructure students' view of general education as "something we have to take" or "something we have to get out of the way before we study what is important—the major," Bowling Green State University, for example, has translated its mission into learning outcome statements so that students develop a common understanding of what the university expects them to learn. These outcomes are also integrated into students' major programs of study and into the cocurriculum (Student Achievement Assessment Committee, Bowling Green State University 2009).

Examining how and where students find opportunities to learn, practice, and reflect on these outcomes is another way an institution translates general education into the fabric of institutional life. Curricular and cocurricular maps can provide a visual representation by charting the courses, educational experiences, and ways of teaching and learning that contribute to students' achievement of these learning outcomes. For physics, as an example, a curricular map illustrates how general education outcomes are woven into a physics curriculum and continually assessed so that students continue to practice and achieve general education outcomes within the major. In short, major programs of study should offer students opportunities over time to transfer, integrate, apply, and practice their general education outcomes.

Chronologically Reinforcing General Education Outcomes throughout Undergraduate Education

Orienting students to general education outcomes and continuing to connect students to these outcomes in their major programs of study contribute to students' ownership of this core learning, as well as to their deepened understanding of the relevance of general education. First-year experiences offer an initial occasion to orient students to general education learning outcomes. Chronological reinforcement occurs through the advising process and through syllabi that identify outcomes specifically addressed in general education courses and in courses in students' majors. Students need to develop an understanding of these outcomes over time, but without multiple opportunities to learn, relearn, and practice these outcomes, these expectations are not likely to become a part of their enduring learning.

Syllabi represent the threads that link students to general education outcomes. Specifically, each syllabus should describe: (1) learning outcomes for a course that align with department or general education outcomes; (2) teaching/learning strategies that promote each learning outcome; and (3) chronological assignments (and methods of assessment) through which students will demonstrate their progress toward or achievement of outcomes. This form of intentional reinforcement of general education learning outcomes throughout all courses keeps students connected to and engaged with the curriculum and cocurriculum.

Altogether, then, articulating general education learning outcomes, mapping those outcomes, and threading them across syllabi serve three important functions, which are enumerated below.

1. They build understanding among faculty in a department and program about the progression, content, topics, pedagogy, and modes of delivery that individual faculty members use to foster agreed-upon learning outcomes. Moreover, such articulation builds understanding across an institution about how programs and departments foster institution-level outcomes, such as their core curriculum or general education outcomes—outcomes that are desirable for graduates from any program.
2. They help students understand over time how "things fit together" across learning experiences inside and outside of the classroom. Students should be enabled to articulate the fruits of their learning, including what they have accomplished and where they have fallen short. And students should become chronologically accountable and responsible for demonstrating desired outcomes along the course of their educational journey as well as at the end of their journey.
3. They provide external parties—such as accreditors, parents, or transfer institutions— evidence of intentional curricular and cocurricular commitment to fostering levels of agreed-upon outcomes.

A Student-Centered Approach to Assessment

A commitment to deepening students' understanding of the relevance of general education outcomes is central to a student-centered approach. To that end, strong general education programs build in opportunities for students to reflect on their learning, including identifying strengths and weaknesses. To assist this process, effective general education programs develop and apply scoring rubrics or use existing ones such as the national rubrics developed under AAC&U's Valid Assessment of Learning in Undergraduate Education project. These offer criteria of judgment that faculty, peers, and students may apply to their work.

ALVERNO COLLEGE
MILWAUKEE, WISCONSIN

Integrating Assessment in Learning

Alverno has a strong "ability-based education" system that requires students to demonstrate competency in a particular area through assessments collected in a learning portfolio. The college does not use traditional assessments like exams, and students track their progress through a digital portfolio system that includes feedback from professors, outside experts, and peers. Faculty feedback and students' own reflection on their work creates "a continuous process that improves learning and integrates it with assessment."

For example, accompanying the work students produce for an electronic portfolio, self-reflective entries should describe how particular work samples represent achievement or progress toward the institution's general education outcomes. Self-reflection reinforces learning by engaging learners in focused thinking about their understanding and misunderstanding. In addition, feedback from multiple individuals—faculty members, staff members, peers, internship advisers, outside reviewers, or representatives from a profession—provides students with realistic responses to their work, causing them to reflect further on their achievement. By contrast, limited feedback, coupled with little opportunity for students to self-reflect on their development or understanding, may contribute to some students' inability to understand and attest to the learning described in institutional outcome statements. And because different individuals learn differently over time, the loss of the opportunity for reflection is not easily made up. Some of the most powerful assessment models for general education outcomes are flexible and individually oriented, allowing students to demonstrate their progress when they are ready, rather than through traditional exams. Alverno College has a well-developed "ability-based education" system that requires demonstrations of student learning in action through course-based and integrative assessments collected in a student portfolio. Faculty and expert feedback, as well as students' own reflections on their learning, help "create a continuous process that improves learning and integrates it with assessment" (Alverno College).

Direct and Indirect Assessment to Ascertain the Efficacy of General Education

Curricular and cocurricular maps not only represent how general education intentions are woven into courses and other educational opportunities; they also provide a framework for collecting, analyzing, and interpreting student achievement along the continuum of students' learning to identify patterns of weakness in student work. Without periodic evidence, we can provide only anecdotes about student learning and "hope" that learning is taking place. Evidence of student learning along their continuum of learning is thus essential.

More to the point, without direct evidence of students' learning represented in their work or performance, we cannot know how effective our collective efforts are. Direct evidence consists of work that students produce to demonstrate their progress toward or achievement of general education outcomes. Case studies, tests, milestone examinations, performances, visual representations, multimedia products, laboratory reports, and collaborative Web sites (such as student-generated wikis) represent some examples of direct methods.

In contrast with closed-ended tests, which seek only yes-or-no responses, educators may use open-ended scoring rubrics such as those developed under AAC&U's VALUE project to identify patterns of strength and weakness in student work. Applied chronologically to samples of student work, scoring rubrics identify how well students are improving or making progress in their learning or identify continued obstacles or challenges students face.

For example, Clarke College, a small Catholic liberal arts college in Iowa, has identified three points along students' college careers at which to collect, analyze, and interpret the achievement of general education outcomes: in an initial cornerstone general education course, at the midpoint in students' major programs of study, and at the end point within students' senior capstone projects. Documenting patterns of strength and weakness in their students' achievement of outcomes enables faculty members to identify alternative pedagogies or educational practices intended to improve student performance.

Learning from students about how they are experiencing the general education curriculum and how they are making meaning of their coursework and educational experience is an essential component of the assessment process as well. Indirect assessment methods capture students' perceptions of their learning and the efficacy of educational practices. By comparing the results of direct methods to results of indirect methods, such as surveys, questionnaires, and interviews, educators can gain a deeper understanding of patterns of student achievement. For instance, joining the results of an online questionnaire that asks students to identify the effectiveness of components of their general education program with the results of sampled student work may shed valuable light on such patterns. In addition, the commitment to eliciting student responses can in itself demonstrate that an institution or program values its learners' perspectives.

> **CLARKE COLLEGE**
> DUBUQUE, IOWA
>
> **Continuous Assessment**
>
> Clarke College collects and analyzes the achievement of learning outcomes at three points in students' academic careers: in an initial cornerstone general education course, at the midpoint of students' major program, and during senior capstone projects. This approach not only allows faculty to assess students' individual progress, but also provides data about the effectiveness of pedagogical methods and practices and lends itself to continuous improvement at the program level.

Using Assessment Results to Improve Student Learning

Educators who offer strong general education programs share an openness to learning about the effectiveness of educational practices through the assessment process. Without this openness, recording patterns of student achievement can become an empty bureaucratic process. Determining that 75 percent of students have satisfactorily demonstrated a general education outcome represents a commitment to accountability. But a commitment to identifying patterns of strength and weakness in that 75 percent, as well as in the remaining 25 percent, and to discovering the reasons for those patterns represents openness to learn more about the teaching/learning process and ways to improve it.

By identifying misunderstandings, misconceptions, flawed reasoning, or an inability to apply previous learning in new contexts, for instance, analysts can track patterns of weakness appearing in student work. Having identified such patterns and reached some understanding as to why they may exist, educators position themselves to consider ways to improve pedagogy, to revise instructional design, or to make modifications in the curriculum design, either by developing indigenous responses or by identifying and adapting salutary practices. Having agreed on necessary changes, educators can then implement them and assess their efficacy.

As a rule of thumb, institutions with strong general education programs will
1. identify one or more learning outcomes they will assess each year;
2. collect evidence of students' progress toward these outcomes;
3. apply scoring rubrics or other gauges of work against benchmarks;

4. identify patterns of weakness that need to be addressed through alternative ways of teaching and learning, instructional design, modes of delivery, and other educational practices;
5. implement agreed-upon changes; and
6. reenter the assessment cycle to ascertain how well changes have improved student learning.

As is characteristic of professionals in any field, competent educators position themselves to become learners about their work. The results of their investigations position them to identify new or improved ways to teach or position students to learn. A strong general education program, then, builds in cycles of inquiry about the efficacy of educational practices. That is, its relevance, vitality, and efficacy are regularly investigated.

Part Four: Sustaining General Education Programs

Chapter 7
Institutional Commitment
Paul L. Gaston

General education programs that continue to grow in strength and effectiveness depend on the friendly scrutiny and dedicated support of faculty members, administrators, and the university community as a whole.

Effective general education programs are not machines. They are organisms that require nurturing if they are to flourish. They reach maturity; unless attended to, they grow stale. If neglected or ignored, they grow weak. Strong programs, by contrast, exemplify the benefits of continuing attention, strong support, and broadly shared responsibility—they are taught with energy, topics are fresh, pedagogy is innovative, and students are engaged. The most effective programs express three key assumptions. First, colleges and universities that offer strong general education programs inevitably embody a commitment to the holistic liberal learning of all students. Second, their faculty members, whatever their discipline or curricular focus, embrace and pursue a broadly shared commitment to assuring that all students benefit from such an education. Finally, many strong colleges and universities discover within these two commitments a signal element in the character of their institutions, a "signature" that helps to define who they are and what they stand for.

Liberal Learning without the Silos

An important emphasis of our survey has been general education's critical—but partial—role in assuring liberal learning. A curriculum has many parts, and all must contribute to the accomplishment of liberal learning objectives if they are to be met. But the "parts" that students bring to their education are much less clearly discrete. While academic programs may reflect divisions between general education and the major and among the sciences, the humanities, the arts, and the social sciences, students' experiences and perspectives are not similarly divided. Or at least they should not be. Facilitators of strong programs consider how best to offer learning that is holistic, associative, and thoughtfully integrated.

A new initiative from the College of Liberal Arts and Sciences at Villanova University well expresses this commitment. Referring to an "interconnected world," the college has created the Villanova Center for Liberal Education, "an innovative academic center dedicated to interdisciplinary teaching, research, and learning in the liberal arts for undergraduate students." Seeking to bring Villanova students "into an ongoing dialogue with some of the College's finest teacher–scholars," the center is intended to "provide a valuable forum for faculty to contribute to their profession, inspire students to become more active and engaged participants in the learning process, and advance the importance of the liberal arts" (Villanova College of Liberal Arts and Sciences). By so doing, the center extends the university's Core Humanities Program, which offers required courses such as an Augustine and Culture seminar that seeks to introduce students to "the life of the mind."

Just as strong general education programs can prompt greater awareness of the transcendent values of liberal learning, so, too, can a holistic approach to liberal learning draw attention to the increasing artificiality of disciplinary boundaries within the academy. Students entering college now bring extensive experience with online data, which is profoundly associative. Google "Lincoln" to research the Gettysburg Address and you may find yourself wanting to learn about a university in the southeast corner of Pennsylvania committed to instruction that is "holistic" and to "challenging students to utilize all levels of cognition" through "holistic" instruction (Lincoln University 2000).

As the Association of American Colleges and Universities essential learning outcomes emphasize, the broader goals of liberal learning can finally be accomplished only through integration and synthesis. The "intellectual and practical skills" that denote a liberally educated individual must be "practiced extensively *across the curriculum.*" Integrative learning must span "general and specialized studies." And a sense of personal and social responsibility must arise through "active involvement with diverse communities and real-world challenges" (AAC&U 2007, 12). Bringing together all these critical elements requires leadership at all levels throughout an institution.

Liberal Learning "Takes a University"

Our review of the essential elements of strong general education programs must include an appreciation of the role played by the individual faculty member—*every* faculty member, whatever the discipline, whatever the course level taught—in making available to all students the benefits of liberal learning. In short, every member of the faculty, whatever his or her field of expertise, contributes to the liberal learning of every student. For good or for ill. Period.

This recognition appears most vividly in the examples of those faculty members who teach not only particular elements characteristic of a liberal learning, but also the values of liberal learning itself. Such faculty members may be found in every discipline and at every level of the curriculum. They teach by precept and by example, through their syllabi, their conduct of their classes, their writing, even their behavior, within and beyond the walls of the institution.

But other members of the faculty may offer a different lesson. While they may be principled, knowledgeable, and professional, they may offer their students the powerful message that the institution's liberal learning goals are, at best, a harmless diversion and, at worst, a meaningless distraction. Unfortunately, as the superb study by former Harvard President Derek Bok (2006) indicates, students are most likely to experience such negative contributions to their liberal learning within their majors, in their third and fourth years, when they tend to have become more clearly focused, more self-interested, and more highly motivated. If the senior faculty who students encounter during this critical period fail to reinforce the liberal learning values introduced through general education, they inevitably undermine such values and may even reverse the best efforts of those who have earlier attempted to teach them. Writing in the *Chronicle Review*, Stanley N. Katz observes, with thinly veiled acrimony, "Our research faculty members have little interest in joining efforts to build core or general-education programs, much less in teaching in them. Moreover, can we be confident that those prized faculty recruits are sufficiently liberally educated to participate in general education?" (2005, B6).

Yet whether the problem is endemic within an institution or atypical, the damage to liberal learning that can be done by an indifferent, hostile, or inappropriately prepared instructor is considerable. Such damage can take many forms.

Overt disregard for the aims of liberal learning is perhaps the least perilous to students. They can recognize narrow obsession when they see it. Faculty members whose authority and personal appeal camouflage a narrow and illiberal approach to learning represent a far greater threat. The accounting professor who never refers to the ethical issues raised by the Enron scandal, or to the contribution of double-entry bookkeeping to the Industrial Revolution, or to Joseph Conrad's vision of competent accounting amid the hell of the "Heart of Darkness" is offering a powerful perspective on liberal learning: namely, that its values are irrelevant to the matter at hand. Similarly, a professor of nineteenth-century history who fails to mention the importance within his period of new accounting techniques, the impact of economic theory on political balances of power, or the ways in which the Industrial Revolution in England stimulated an increase in small businesses sends the same message: my discipline, as I understand and profess it, is what matters—is *all* that matters.

To be sure, some professors avoid ethical issues or other questions of value because they lack confidence in addressing issues beyond the boundaries of their respective disciplines. Others may hold that the important advances in their fields are directly attributable to the focus that results from specialization. Still others may claim that their obligation to cover and impart a broad field of information precludes the allocation of class time to matters not clearly included in the syllabus.

Each of these concerns has some merit. But institutions that promise the benefits of a liberal learning have a responsibility to address them. Those who remain resolutely within their disciplinary silos out of a sense of professional responsibility should be reminded that their responsibility includes modeling the benefits of liberal learning. That includes a willingness to consider issues and contexts that bear on the subject being taught. When professors avoid issues of value or ignore perspectives that add depth, liberal learning suffers. Those who attribute the productivity of their discipline to its specificity should be encouraged to engage in dialogue with specialists in other disciplines.

The damage to liberal learning that can be done by an indifferent, hostile, or inappropriately prepared instructor is considerable.

While important advances may be attributed to academic specialization, colleges and universities that aspire to provide their students with a liberal learning must not depend on their students to create a coherent educational experience from their encounters with a succession of specialists. And those who insist that their obligation for "coverage" requires an unblinking determination to deliver all that is expected should be made acquainted with the profound paradigm shift in our academic generation, from a focus on the techniques of teaching to an emphasis on facilitating, confirming, and improving learning. As has become clear, this shift need not lead to neglect of course objectives; to the contrary, it requires their clarification. Nor does it ignore the development of competencies among students; it ensures that students are in fact developing competencies. And, most important for those concerned with liberal learning, an emphasis on learning rather than teaching respects students as whole individuals with an impressive capacity for making connections, drawing analogies, and finding associations.

More subtle, and therefore perhaps even more damaging, may be the faculty member who is unable or unwilling to model the ordinary interests, sympathies, or native awareness of the liberally educated individual. A statewide leader in library science convened a meeting at 10:00 a.m. on September 11, 2001, by which time it was evident that a catastrophe of unprecedented proportions was taking place. By his resolute insistence that the agenda for the day be "covered," regardless of what might be happening in the world, he offered an indelible lesson in insensitivity and disproportion. He failed even to realize the particular relevance for librarians in the unfolding of the disaster. There were similar stories from classrooms in many a college and university at the time, where the emphasis on delivering the prepared knowledge overwhelmed attention to the more powerful learning from that day.

The bright side of this coin is the good news that lies in the opportunity every member of the academic community has to further the liberal learning of students. Whatever their discipline, faculty members, student affairs professionals, and indeed everyone within an institution can contribute to its liberal learning goals.

Such opportunity begins most clearly with those courses most traditionally associated with liberal learning, those that directly address broadly agreed-upon goals for twenty-first-century learning. Courses addressing these goals must of course be taught effectively by faculty members who embrace the values and vision they express. Just because a course belongs to a core curriculum offers no guarantee that it will contribute to the liberal learning of students; a course in the fine arts, or theology, or the development of Western civilization may operate within a confined perspective, just as may a course in organic chemistry or finance. Similarly, a course that falls outside of the core curriculum may offer a uniquely liberating experience for some students.

Ultimately, institutions must recognize that the offering of effective core curriculum courses by enlightened and dedicated faculty members, whether they be traditional liberal arts courses or not, should be only a beginning, for faculty members have a responsibility to teach the values of liberal learning whenever they teach, whatever they teach. A thoughtfully planned, discerning, and coherent general education program, whether limited to the first two years of the curriculum or distributed throughout the baccalaureate, can go a long way toward supporting faculty effectiveness. But faculty members also create learning (or fail to do so) by pursuing liberal learning objectives through courses within their disciplines, by the breadth (or narrowness) of their intellectual interests, by their enthusiasm (or lack of enthusiasm) for the life of the college or university as a whole, and by their intellectual engagement (or the lack of it) with disciplines other than their own.

Eight Practical Approaches

What does this mean in practical terms? Any institution intent on providing its students with the benefits of a liberal learning will address this question in its own way. But it is possible to suggest eight practical steps that we as faculty members can take to ensure that a shared commitment to the values of liberal learning makes a difference for our students.

1. **Break out of the silos.** We can expand our awareness of the "liberal" dimensions of the courses within our respective disciplines, both those offered within the core curriculum and those reserved for majors. Much exciting scholarship is appearing on the margins between our areas of expertise, but we may have to seek out the less traditional venues in which it is appearing in order to find it. Doing so would be very much worth our while. We are likely to become better informed, more enthusiastic, and more effective educators. We may even become more expert as specialists.

2. **Model commitment to general education with colleagues.** We can share with our students and colleagues the fruits of our liberal learning and encourage our colleagues and students to do the same. A professor of English who comments in class (or a faculty meeting) on a recent article in *Scientific American*, an economist who mentions a perceptive review of a Bruce Springsteen concert, or a biologist who begins a class on chlorophyll by reading (or reciting from memory) Robert Frost's "Nothing Gold Can Stay" will create a positive and indelible impression while prompting genuine learning. Walker Percy, the novelist and essayist, once observed that the most profound learning occurs when conventional expectations collapse: the biology student one day finds a sonnet taped to her lab table, while the literature student receives a set of dissecting tools and a dogfish shark in a pan.

3. **Establish clear liberal education goals for each course**. We should establish clear learning goals—including liberally educative ones—for each course that we teach. Such goals should be stated explicitly in the syllabus, in lesson outlines, and during each class meeting. A teacher of Shakespeare might schedule a discussion of Elizabethan science and finance. A teacher of finance might want to reach out to a colleague to share a discussion of *The Merchant of Venice*. If there are unavoidable constraints that will prevent our addressing certain liberal dimensions of our subjects, we can at least acknowledge them, offer pointers for self-guided study, and refer students to more inclusive courses.

4. **Be flexible and relevant.** We can exercise logistical and intellectual flexibility by responding to emerging issues, especially when they are germane to what we are teaching, but occasionally even when they are not. Some issues are so compelling that to ignore them in any classroom is to make oneself peripheral to the educational process. Tsunamis, terrorist attacks, or earthquakes are not just newsworthy disasters but are also opportunities for reflective response.
5. **Allow students to own their learning.** We can empower our students in the development of their liberal learning by sharing to some degree the ownership of our courses. At a minimum, we can structure some time in each class session for student observations related but perhaps tangential to the issues formally scheduled for discussion. And we might allow at least one or two class sessions during each course for the pursuit of emphases that emerge in the course or that students are defining as emergent. A gifted teacher of calculus at the University of Tennessee at Chattanooga would demonstrate even to novices the mathematical underpinnings of everything from Nolan Ryan's curve ball to missions of the space shuttle.
6. **Promote liberal learning in everyday life.** We can promote opportunities for liberal learning outside of the classroom. Acquainting our students with the educational and cultural opportunities on campus and in the community would be a start. Sharing our own enthusiasm for particular scheduled events would be even more persuasive. And actually showing up would be most effective. The sociology professor who attends a lecture on liquid crystal physics will probably learn something she did not know. (She might also enjoy startling a scientific colleague by her presence.) And her students will profit from her example.
7. **Highlight relationships between topics and disciplines.** We can seek opportunities with colleagues, especially those in other disciplines, to discover, define, and highlight relations among the courses we are teaching. The process of association itself is liberally educative, and it should be apparent that the broader and more interesting the contexts, the more likely it is that genuine learning will take place. We can also encourage our students to extend our efforts by asking difficult questions and by volunteering their own developing intellectual enthusiasms.
8. **Exemplify engaged lifelong learning to students.** Above all, as privileged members of the academy, we can offer ourselves in all that we do as energetic learners. We can attend courses offered by colleagues. (Indiana University once encouraged this practice by offering incentives.) We can invite our colleagues to attend our courses and to raise questions with us. We can ask colleagues and students for reading suggestions and report back on our experiences. We can seek guest lecturers and discussants. We can take a hike and report on the ferns we identified. We can follow the instructions in *Scientific American* to perform a simple acoustical experiment. Whatever our field or primary expertise, as we share with our students and colleagues the richness of our intellectual experience, we model for them the fruits of a liberal learning and, above all, testify to its value in our lives.

Faculty members who embrace in full the values of a liberal learning can offer their students an intense and indelible experience. They may also approach an ideal that, in all likelihood, has rarely been attained. What is certain is that if a college or university is to honor its stated mission of offering a liberal learning to its students, the engagement of every member of the faculty is essential.

General Education as "Signature"

Some colleges and universities still view general education as a mandate to be fulfilled rather than as an opportunity to be grasped and turned into an advantage. Faculty, students, and advisers in such institutions tend to agree: general education is a requirement to be "gotten out of the way" so that serious study in the major may begin.

But many others, including those whose accomplishments are cited in these pages, have indeed grasped the opportunity of general education reform in order to develop offerings that are compelling for the faculty, attractive to students, and competitive in the higher education marketplace. In short, exceptional general education programs distinguish institutions and enable them to define themselves more fully and more positively. As Stephen L. Trainor, former dean of undergraduate studies at Salve Regina University, wrote, such programs capture "the distinctive mission and essence of an institution" (2004, 16). The benefits—for student success, faculty recruitment, alumni support, public awareness—can be considerable.

We have noted many of the elements characteristic of effective general education programs, but a few additional examples of curricula that represent institutional "signatures" may provide an appropriate peroration to this brief summons to excellence.

We might well begin with Salve Regina and the lessons its experience offers. Determined to avoid "a least-common-denominator model designed to offend no one" (Trainor 2004, 16), the university sought consensus for a counter-intuitive process relying heavily on definition of "the problem," strategies for drawing on faculty creativity, rubrics for evaluating alternate models, and the identification and implementation of the most compelling one. The "high-profile" result of the process is a core of required courses intended to "foster discussion and lively debate" among learners "working for a world that is harmonious, just and merciful" (Trainor 2004, 17). Offerings within the core include required courses such as What It Means to Be Human; Seeking Wisdom: From Wonder to Justice; and Christianity in Dialogue with World Religions. A capstone called Living Wisdom, Contemporary Challenges captures the essence of a curriculum that is distinctive, clearly aligned with the values of the university, and expressive of its culture—in short, a "signature."

On the other end of the higher education spectrum, a large public flagship, the University of Maryland, began in the spring of 2010 to move toward a signature program by offering "signature courses" according to several "I" categories. Intended as precursors to a new, distinctive general education offering, the new courses "are designed to *investigate* significant issues with *imagination* and *intellect* with a belief that they will *inspire* future investigation and provide concrete mechanisms to *implement innovative* ideas" (University of Maryland 2009). Courses on subjects ranging from Shakespeare (Acting Human) to the Chesapeake Bay (Intersection of Science, Economics, and Policy) to the threat of asteroid impact (Collisions in Space) are meant to offer students "not only new intellectual domains to explore but also new ways to think about contemporary problems like the energy crisis and age old dilemmas like ecological sustainability" (University of Maryland 2009).

Michigan State University's claim to a "signature program" rests, in part, on three centers for integrative studies, one in arts and humanities, one in general science, and one in social science. Through these centers, students pursue courses "that integrate multiple ways of knowing into an enhanced appreciation of our humanity, creativity, knowledge, and responsibilities for ourselves and our world" (Michigan State University Centers for Integrative Studies). A sampling of the course titles suggests that the creative claims for the program are expressed through the opportunities it offers: Human Values and the Arts and Humanities; Music and Society in the Modern World; Roles of Language in Society; Visions of the University; Concepts of Reality through Physical Science; Power, Authority, and Exchange; and Society and the Individual.

In Sum

Other examples of effective practice could easily be given. But the point is made. One important way that colleges and universities may distinguish themselves and enhance their competitiveness on many stages—that of public accountability, that of student recruitment, and that of alumni support, to name a few—is to reach consensus on the goals of liberal learning and to move intentionally to align their general education, major, and cocurricular offerings with those goals. Effective institutions then measure the quality of their programming through assiduous and creative assessment. And, most important, they use what they learn to make themselves even more effective.

But the end of such efforts finally transcends issues of institutional prominence or competitiveness. Clarifying the goals of liberal learning and strengthening general education finally has one overriding objective: to support students in their learning and to enable them to achieve successful careers and satisfying lives.

References

Adelman, C. 1999. *Answers in the tool box: Academic intensity, attendance patterns, and bachelor's degree attainment.* Washington, DC: U.S. Department of Education.

Alverno College. Ability-based curriculum. www.alverno.edu/about_alverno/ability_curriculum.html.

American Association of University Professors. 2009. On the brink: 2008-09 report on the economic status of the profession. *Academe* 95 (2): 14–93.

Association of American Colleges. 1985. *Integrity in the college curriculum.* Washington, DC: Association of American Colleges.

———. 1988. *A new vitality in general education.* Washington, DC: Association of American Colleges.

———. 1994. *Strong foundations: Twelve principles for effective general education programs.* Washington, DC: Association of American Colleges.

Association of American Colleges and Universities. 2002. *Greater expectations: A new vision for learning as a nation goes to college.* Washington, DC: Association of American Colleges and Universities.

———. 2005. *Liberal education outcomes: A preliminary report on student achievement in college.* Washington, DC: Association of American Colleges and Universities.

———. 2007. *College learning for the new global century: A report from the National Leadership Council for Liberal Education and America's Promise.* Washington, DC: Association of American Colleges and Universities.

Bauerlein, M. 2009. The state of general education. *Chronicle of Higher Education,* September 9. www.chronicle.com/blogPost/The-State-of-General-Education/7899/.

Blaich, C., and K. Wise. 2009. *Overview of findings from the first year of the Wabash National Study of Liberal Arts Education.* Wabash, Indiana: Wabash Center of Inquiry. www.liberalarts.wabash.edu/storage/Overview_of_Findings_from_the_First_Year_web_07.17.09.pdf.

Bok, D. 2006. *Our underachieving colleges.* Princeton, NJ: Princeton University Press.

Bresciani, M. J., and J. A. Anderson. n.d. General education assessment: A brief overview. www.ncsu.edu/assessment/ger/assess_gen_ed_pres.pdf.

Brown Office of the Dean of the College. 2008. Liberal learning at Brown. www.brown.edu/Administration/Dean_of_the_College/curriculum/downloads/Lib_Learning_Goals.pdf.

Carnegie Foundation for the Advancement of Teaching. U.S. Professors of the Year Awards Program. www.usprofessorsoftheyear.org/index.cfm.

Carnevale, A., and D. Humphreys. 2010. The economic value of liberal education. Presentation at the annual meeting of the Association of American Colleges and Universities, Washington, DC.

Center for Education and the Workforce. 2009. *College is still the best option.* Washington, DC: Center for Education and the Workforce.

Dillon, S. 2010. High schools to offer plan to graduate 2 years early. *New York Times,* February 17, A14.

Donnelly-Smith, L. 2008. Enhancing intentionality in the requirement-free curriculum. *Peer Review* 10 (4): 9–11.

Gaston, P. L., and J. G. Gaff. 2009. *Revising general education—and avoiding the potholes: A guide for curricular change.* Washington, DC: Association of American Colleges and Universities.

Gaston, P. L. 2010. *The challenge of Bologna: What United States higher education has to learn from Europe, and why it matters that we learn it.* Sterling, VA: Stylus Publishers.

Hart Research Associates. 2009. *Trends and emerging practices in general education.* Washington, DC: Association of American Colleges and Universities. www.aacu.org/membership/documents/2009MemberSurvey_Part2.pdf.

Hart Research Associates. 2010. *Raising the bar: Employers' views on college learning in the wake of the economic downturn.* Washington, DC: Association of American Colleges and Universities. www.aacu.org/leap/documents/2009_EmployerSurvey.pdf.

Huber, M. and P. Hutchings. 2004. *Integrative learning: Mapping the terrain.* Washington, DC: Association of American Colleges and Universities.

Hu, S., and G. D. Kuh. 2003. Diversity experiences and college student learning and personal development. *Journal of College Student Development* 44(3): 320–34.

Katz, S. 2005. Liberal education on the ropes. *Chronicle Review* 51 (30): B6.

Kirk, K. Experience-based environmental projects. *Pedagogy in Action: The SERC Portal for Educators.* http://serc.carleton.edu/sp/library/enviroprojects/index.html.

Kuh, G. D. 2008. *High-impact educational practices: What they are, who has access to them, and why they matter.* Washington, DC: Association of American Colleges and Universities.

Lattuca, L., and J. Stark. 2009. *Shaping the college curriculum.* 2nd ed. San Francisco: Jossey-Bass.

Light, R. J. 2001. *Making the most of college: Students speak their minds.* Cambridge, MA: Harvard University Press.

Lincoln University. 2000. University philosophy statements. www.lincoln.edu/president/stratplanphilosophy.htm.

Maki, P. L. 2004. *Assessing for learning: Building a sustainable commitment across the institution.* Sterling, VA: Stylus Publishing.

Michigan State University Centers for Integrative Studies. Michigan State University integrative studies. www.ns.msu.edu/cisgs/CISGSHOMEPAGE/brochure.html.

Mississippi Economic Council. 2009. Millsaps College named to president's honor roll for service. News release, March 4. www.msmec.com/mx/hm.asp?id=millsapshonor.

Musil, C.M., with M. García, Y. T. Moses, and D. G. Smith. 1995. *Diversity in higher education: A work in progress.* Washington, DC: Association of American Colleges and Universities.

Ohio State University. Service-learning initiative: Elements of a service-learning course. http://service-learning.osu.edu/docs/elements_SLCourse.pdf

Orszag, J. M., P. R. Orszag, and D. M. Whitmore. 2001. *Learning and earning: Working in college.* Washington, DC: Sebago Associates, Inc. www.nsea.info/docs/services/resources/Upromise.doc.

Otterbein College. Integrative studies program. www.otterbein.edu/IS/mission-history.asp.

Peter D. Hart Research Associates. 2007. *How should colleges prepare students to succeed in today's global economy?* Washington, DC: Peter D. Hart Research Associates. www.aacu.org/leap/documents/Re8097abcombined.pdf.

Portland State University. Senior capstone courses. www.pdx.edu/unst/senior-capstone-courses.

Rhodes College. 2007. *The foundations curriculum.* www.rhodes.edu/images/content/College_Catalogue/foundations.curriculum.pdf.

Rhodes, Terrel L. 2010. *Assessing outcomes and improving achievement: Tips and tools for using rubrics.* Washington, DC: Association of American Colleges and Universities.

Saint Louis Community College. General education. www.stlcc.edu/Programs/General_Education/.

Strauss, W., and N. Howe. 2003. *Millennials go to college: Strategies for a new generation on campus.* Washington, DC: American Association of Collegiate Registrars.

Student Achievement Assessment Committee, Bowling Green State University. 2009. University Learning Outcomes. www.bgsu.edu/offices/assessment/page31434.html.

Trainor, S. L. 2004. Designing a signature general education program. *Peer Review* 7 (1): 16–19

Tulane University. Public service graduation requirement. http://tulane.edu/cps/about/graduation-requirement.cfm.

U.S. Department of Education, National Center for Education Statistics. 2007. 2003–04 *Beginning postsecondary students longitudinal study, first follow-up* (BPS:04/06). Washington, DC: U.S. Government Printing Office.

———. 2008. 2007–08 *National postsecondary student aid study* (NPSAS:08). Washington, DC: U.S. Government Printing Office.

———. 2009. *The Condition of Education 2009* (NCES 2009-081). Washington, DC: U.S. Government Printing Office.

University of Maryland. 2009. The "I" series: Signature courses for the pilot for general education at the University of Maryland, spring 2010. www.provost.umd.edu/SP07/Implement/I-Series_Brochure.pdf.

University of Nebraska–Lincoln. 2008. Achievement-centered education: Institutional objectives and student learning outcomes. ace.unl.edu/PDFs/ace1_IOSLO.pdf.

Venezia, A., M. W. Krist, and A. L. Antonio. 2004. *Betraying the college dream: How disconnected K-12 and postsecondary education systems undermine student aspirations.* www.stanford.edu/group/bridgeproject/betrayingthecollegedream.pdf.

Villanova College of Liberal Arts and Sciences. Villanova Center for Liberal Education. www.villanova.edu/artsci/vcle/about/.

Wesch, M. 2007. A vision of students today. 4 min, 44 sec. video. http://mediatedcultures.net/ksudigg/?p=119.

Willamette University. 2001. *Towards a powerful co-curriculum: A report from the Task Force on Campus Life.* Salem, OR: Willamette University.

Willamette University Office of Campus Life. Kaneko commons: Living. Learning. Leadership. www.willamette.edu/dept/campuslife/res_commons/kaneko/.

About the Author

PAUL L. GASTON is Trustees Professor at Kent State University, an appointment that calls for teaching and research in at least two different disciplines—in his case, higher education and English literature. He concluded twenty-five years as an academic administrator by serving as provost of Kent State from 1999 to 2007. He earned the PhD and MA in English from the University of Virginia, where he was a Woodrow Wilson Fellow and a DuPont Fellow. He has written extensively on subjects ranging from interart analogies, the poetry of George Herbert, and the fiction of Walker Percy, to academic strategic planning, the Higher Education Act, and computer-dominated futures trading. His most recent books are *Revising General Education—And Avoiding the Potholes: A Guide for Curricular Change* (with Jerry G. Gaff) (AAC&U, 2009), and *The Challenge of Bologna: What United States Higher Education Has to Learn from Europe and Why It Matters That We Learn It* (Stylus, 2010). Gaston has served on the faculty of the AAC&U Institute on General Education since 2001 and works frequently as a consultant to colleges, universities, and accrediting associations.